Eve[...] wit[...]

SEP[...]

CW01640918

The Way of Simplicity

'Love the Lord your God... Love your neighbour as yourself'
Mark 12:30–31

Selwyn Hughes
Revised and updated by Mick Brooks

CWR, Waverley Abbey House, Waverley Lane, Farnham, Surrey GU9 8EP, UK **Tel: 01252 784700**
Email: mail@cwr.org.uk Registered Charity No. 294387. Registered Limited Company No. 1990308.

Cover image: Sonja Lekovic/Stocksy
Quiet Time image: pixabay.com
Printed in England by Linney Print

CWR

FSC www.fsc.org MIX Paper from responsible sources FSC® C015900

Every Day with Jesus is available in large print from CWR. It is also available on **audio and DAISY** in the UK and Eire for the sole use of those with a visual impairment worse than N12, or who are registered blind. For details please contact **Torch Trust for the Blind**, Tel: 01858 438260. Torch House, Torch Way, Northampton Road, Market Harborough LE16 9HL.

A word of introduction...

Does life sometimes appear too complicated to you? The arguments seem to rage almost daily – convincing us of how complex and complicated day-to-day life has become, when in reality, perhaps we ourselves are making life more complex than it actually is?

Jesus lived in what remains one of the most complex, multi-layered societies in the world – yet among the religious, political and personal tensions, He was able to keep His everyday living focused on life's most fundamental issues. He was able to see past all the 'smoke and mirrors' and focus on what was important. When competing factions conspired to confound Him, He made one of the most profound, challenging and insightful statements. As we read in Matthew 22:34–40, an expert in the Law was commissioned to ask Him, 'what is the greatest commandment?' In that moment, Jesus reduced over 3,000 laws to a simple – but not in any way simplistic – statement: 'Love God and love others as yourself, as all the other laws depend upon these.'

As C.S. Lewis once said: 'Put first things first and we get second things thrown in: put second things first and we lose both first and second things.' It's my hope and prayer that as you meditate on these devotional writings each day, you will discover a new way of simplicity and freedom – able to discard anything that hinders or holds you back.

Mick

Mick Brooks, Consulting Editor

Free small group resources to accompany this issue can be found at www.cwr.org.uk/extra

The *EDWJ* Facebook community is growing!
To join the conversation visit www.facebook.com/edwjpage

The way of simplicity

FOR READING & MEDITATION – 2 CORINTHIANS 11:1–15

'I am afraid… your minds may… be led astray from your sincere and pure devotion to Christ.' (v3)

The theme we are about to explore together – the way of simplicity – first began stirring my spirit some years ago now, when I spoke at a conference in Malaysia. During the conference someone said: 'The Christian way is the way of complete simplicity.' I remember thinking to myself at the time: 'If that's true, why have we made it so complicated?'

No one has been more straightforward than Jesus Himself, and that this probably should be one of the hallmarks of His followers also is brought out in today's passage. The Authorised Version and the New King James Version translate it in what I believe is a much better way than the NIV: 'But I fear, lest somehow, as the serpent deceived Eve by his craftiness, so your minds may be corrupted from the simplicity that is in Christ' (v3, NKJV). Few, I believe, have had a more brilliant intellect than Paul, yet he saw the danger of depending on intellect rather than on Jesus. He highlights that Eve was led away because she put her own reasoning before God's clear instruction. The guidance she and Adam had been given was simple, uncomplicated, and easy to understand, but she allowed the serpent to muddle her thinking. And when wilful action followed wilful thinking, the whole universe was catapulted into what we now describe as 'the Fall'.

FURTHER STUDY

Phil. 3:1–16; Matt. 16:24; Luke 14:33

1. How did Paul consider his own achievements?

2. What was his pursuit in life?

On one level, our faith to which we are called is the simplest thing in all the world – simple without being simplistic. When we take that which is so simple and complicate it by our additions or subtractions, we make it more difficult for ourselves and others to follow. 'The Christian way is the way of complete simplicity.' Why then do we try to complicate it?

Lord God, forgive us that as Your Church we have taken that which You intended to be simple and straightforward and turned it into something so complicated. Help us understand and demonstrate 'the simplicity that is in Christ'. Amen.

'In simplicity sublime'

FOR READING & MEDITATION – MATTHEW 22:23–40

'an expert in the law, tested him... "Teacher, which is the greatest commandment in the Law?"' (vv35–36)

The poet Tennyson, when writing about a close friend, referred to him in these moving words: 'Rich in saving common-sense... In his simplicity sublime.' Whenever I recollect that statement, immediately it reminds me of Jesus. No one has ever demonstrated the sublimity of simplicity more than He. His entrance into this world, for example, was simple. He was born in a humble cattle shed and spent His early years in an inconspicuous village called Nazareth, not as a king or a military commander but as a carpenter.

His words when He started to teach were simple and straightforward too. He used parables that often intrigued and stretched the imagination, but His language was the language of simplicity. His lifestyle, also, was simple and uncomplicated – a complete contrast to that of the Pharisees, which was extremely complex. They lived by all kinds of taboos and regulations and laws. There were about 3,500 regulations that the Pharisees believed they ought to observe in order to be accepted by God.

I wonder if the lawyer who stood up to ask Jesus the question in today's passage realised that Jesus' answer was a stroke of genius. Jesus summarised all the laws and commandments in just two: love God and love others. If, as someone has said, 'Beauty is an absence of superfluities', then there must have been none more beautiful than Jesus Christ – although there may have been no outward beauty to attract us to Him (Isa. 53:2), most certainly there was beauty in His inner character. In Him there was no superfluity or pretence, no useless verbiage, no quibbling or prevaricating. He was perfect in everything. And in simplicity? Sublime.

FURTHER STUDY

Luke 10:25–37; 20:20–26; John 8:1–11

1. In what different ways did people try to catch Jesus out?

2. In what simple but profound ways did He respond?

Sublime Saviour, cleanse me of all complications and ambiguousness, so that I might be as honest and authentic as You were when on earth. This I ask in and through Your precious name. Amen.

Whole facts

FOR READING & MEDITATION – MATTHEW 5:27–37

'And do not swear by your head, for you cannot make even one hair white or black.' (v36)

We said yesterday that life for the Pharisees was extremely complicated, for they lived by innumerable taboos and regulations and laws. Jesus summarised these laws to two: love God and love others also. That is genius. Jesus' response and use of language was a model of simplicity. Let's explore this together over the next few days in order that we might begin to learn and know how to be as simple and straightforward as He was in the way we communicate with others.

Have you ever noticed in reading the Gospels that Jesus' words are stripped of all useless verbiage and are as near to fact as it is possible to get? It was said of Cromwell that his words were 'half battles', meaning that there was power in what he said as well as in what he did. If Cromwell's words were 'half battles' then Jesus' words were and are whole facts. The religious leaders of the day tried to make their language lofty and impressive and give their statements an added gravity by swearing on everything they could think of – everything in heaven and earth. But as we see in today's passage, Jesus told them: 'Do not swear at all: either by heaven, for it is God's throne; or by the earth, for it is his footstool... Simply let your "Yes" be "Yes", and your "No", "No"' (vv35,37).

What He was saying was this – you don't have to strengthen the truth by an oath, trying to get this, that, and the other behind it. The whole universe stands behind it. Live in a way that makes an oath unnecessary. We never see Jesus trying to buttress or reinforce His remarks with an oath. His words were always true and always factual. We too must learn to communicate in this way.

FURTHER STUDY

James 1:19–27;
Prov. 13:3;
21:23;
1 Pet. 3:10

1. What makes religion worthless?
2. What must those do who want to see good days?

Lord God, help me live by this simple rule that my 'Yes' always means 'Yes' and my 'No' always means 'No'. Father, this is how Your Son lived, and I want to live like this also. Help me, dear Lord. In Jesus' name. Amen.

Whole truth

FOR READING & MEDITATION – MATTHEW 5:33–48

'let your "Yes" be "Yes", and your "No", "No"; anything beyond this comes from the evil one.' (v37)

We continue with the same passage that we looked at yesterday because I want to focus on the words that form part of our text for today: 'anything beyond this comes from the evil one.' What Jesus is saying here is that the kingdom of God is built on truth and goodness; the kingdom of darkness is built on lies and deceit.

As we saw yesterday, you don't have to strengthen the truth by an oath, trying to get this, that, and the other behind it, for the universe is already behind the truth. It is self-authenticating. The devil is behind all lies, and in one place Jesus said of him: 'When he lies, he speaks his native language, for he is a liar and the father of lies' (John 8:44). God intended everything for truth, but Satan has so twisted things that now many believe that in order to succeed they have to be prepared to lie occasionally.

One way in which we can describe the difference between Christ's kingdom and the devil's kingdom is to say that one is simple and the other complicated. As Sir Walter Scott observed: 'Oh! What a tangled web we weave, when first we practise to deceive.' Goodness is always a reduction of life to simplicity. Just analyse a lie, for example. Lies are always ambiguous, complicated, and deceiving. Truth is straightforward, uncomplicated, and open. If you lie, you need to have a good memory; you need to remember each time what you have said, and the more you lie, the more anxiety is provoked within you in case you trip yourself up. But if you speak the truth you don't need to remember what you said or how you said it; you simply speak the truth all the time. Jesus spoke the truth, all the time. And following close to Him, so will we.

FURTHER STUDY

2 Cor. 2:1–11; Prov. 12:22; 19:5

1. What was Paul aware of?

2. What does the Lord delight in?

Father, thank You for reminding me that in order to live like Your Son I must stay close to Him. Help me not to depend on myself but depend on Him. In His strong and powerful name I ask it. Amen.

The worst thing...

FOR READING & MEDITATION – LUKE 20:20–26

'Teacher, we know that you... teach the way of God in accordance with the truth.' (v21)

We are seeing that, unlike many of the people of His day and today, Jesus lived a simple and uncomplicated life. Never once did He tell a lie or try to strengthen what He said by an oath. When He said 'Yes' He meant 'Yes', and when He said 'No' He meant 'No'. We learn from today's verse that even Jesus' questioners had to admit that He taught the way of God in accordance with the truth, but behind their very questions was a hidden agenda.

The whole thrust and energy of the universe God designed and created is simple, uncomplicated, and built on truth. There are great mysteries, of course, but no lies. Scientific laws are upheld by truth. Gravity, for example, will not lie; it can be relied upon wherever you are in the world. It has often been said that the word 'evil' is the word 'live' spelt backwards. The devil delights in trying to reverse God's design for living.

The fact that the universe is built to run on truth can be verified by the simple device known as a 'lie detector'. The lie detector test works on the basis that people who tell lies and know they are telling lies become increasingly anxious and uncomfortable, and this anxiety is then picked up by the machine. But why does telling a lie make a person anxious? Because we are built for truth, and any departure from it registers on the inside in a way that can be picked up on the outside. A lie detector is not infallible and can sometimes (though not often) be fooled. But what cannot be fooled is the soul of the person who is lying. The worst thing about being a liar is to be the person telling the lie.

FURTHER STUDY

John 1:1–14; Psa. 119:72; Prov. 23:23; Eph. 6:14

1. What are the elements of Christ's glory?

2. What piece of the Christian's armour holds it all together?

Dear Father, help me lay hold of the fact that a lie diminishes me, but the truth develops me. I cannot live successfully by a lie any more than I can defy gravity. May I be a person of truth. In Jesus' name I pray. Amen.

No need to punctuate

FOR READING & MEDITATION – EPHESIANS 4:17–32

'Do not let any unwholesome talk come out of your mouths' (v29)

We continue meditating on the simple and uncomplicated life of Jesus. He had no need to bolster what He said with loud affirmations and oaths, for everything He said and did was according to the truth.

While on this topic of oaths, allow me to bring into the discussion the whole question of inappropriate language. Several ministers I have talked to over the years have shared with me their concern at the increasing use of unnecessary words and swearing among Christians. These range from crude expressions and expletives to occasional profanities. Prior to my coming to faith I could hardly speak a sentence without punctuating it with some swear-word or blasphemy, but I am grateful that when Christ came into my life one of the first things He did was clean up my language. I have always been intrigued as to why people use such strong swear-words, and I once made a special study of this issue. This is what I found: those who curse and use swear-words are unsure of themselves, so they try to make their statements more emphatic by swearing. Swearing is not a sign of strength, but of weakness. The more you swear, the weaker your statements. Swearing and profanity is often the punctuation people use when they feel unsteady and insecure.

FURTHER STUDY

James 5:1–12;
Lev. 19:12;
James 3:10;
Rom. 12:14

1. What pattern of life does James say we can slip into?

2. What does James admonish us not to do?

Can you imagine a swear-word or a profanity ever crossing the lips of Jesus? I can't. He was secure in the knowledge that He was His Father's Son, and this held Him steady in the ebb and flow of life's events. We are the Father's sons and daughters, and can walk in the light of that fact. If we do, then what need do we have of any more 'punctuation'?

Father God, forgive me if I look to other ways to increase my significance than You. And if my words and language do not reflect my trust in You, then do what is necessary to bring me to the place of dependent trust. In Jesus' name. Amen.

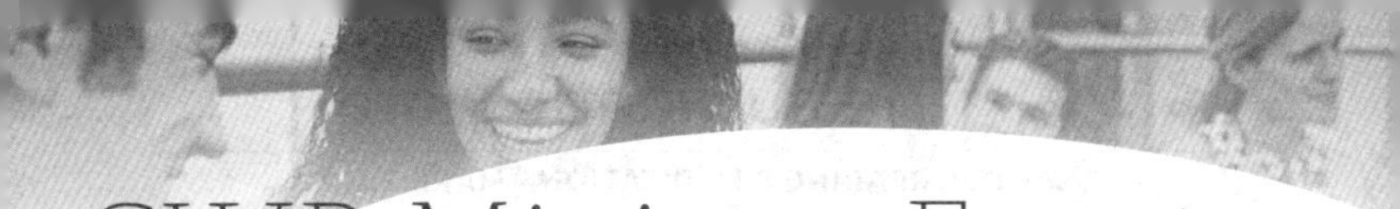

CWR Ministry Events

PLEASE PRAY FOR THE TEAM

DATE	EVENT	PLACE	PRESENTER(S)
7 Sep	Decision Making and the Will of God	Waverley Abbey House	Andy Peck
14 Sep	Small Groups Rebooted	WAH	Andy Peck
16 Sep	Insight into Bereavement	WAH	Peter Jackson
16 Sep	Partners' Day	WAH	CWR team
22–24 Sep	Inspiring Women Autumn Weekend: You Prepare a Table Before Me	WAH	Inspiring Women team
28 Sep	Refreshing Your Devotional Life	WAH	Andy Peck
28 Sep	The Bible in an Evening	WAH	Andy Peck
5 Oct	Introduction to Preaching	WAH	Andy Peck
10 Oct	Inspiring Women Autumn Day: Living in Christ	WAH	Amy Boucher Pye and Inspiring Women team
11–13 Oct	Coaching and Mentoring	WAH	Andy Peck and Beverley Shepherd
14 Oct	Boundaries	WAH	Kara Lawman and team
19 Oct	Pastoral Care Today	WAH	Andy Peck
20–22 Oct	Bible Discovery Weekend: Psalms	WAH	Philip Greenslade
23–27 Oct	Autumn Country Break	Pilgrim Hall	Pilgrim Hall team

Please pray for our students and tutors on our ongoing BA Counselling programme at Waverley Abbey College (which takes place at Waverley Abbey House and Pilgrim Hall), as well as our Certificate and Diploma of Christian Counselling and MA in Christian Counselling qualifications.

We would also appreciate prayer for our ongoing ministry in Singapore and Cambodia, as well as the many regional events that will be happening around the UK this year.

For further information and a full list of CWR's courses, seminars and events, call **+44 (0)1252 784719** or visit **www.cwr.org.uk/courses**

You can also download our free Prayer Track, which includes daily prayers, from **www.cwr.org.uk/free-resources**

The authentic word

FOR READING & MEDITATION – MARK 2:1–12

'and he preached the word to them.' (v2)

I am always fascinated when I read this account in Mark's Gospel. We are told that when Jesus entered a house in Capernaum, people, hearing He was in the home, crowded into the room to listen to what He had to say. He spoke to them, of course, in His usual direct and simple manner, but what intrigues me is the phrase Mark uses to describe this moment: 'He preached the word to them.' What does he mean: 'He preached the word to them'? What was that 'word'? Was it the written Scriptures, the Old Testament?

FURTHER STUDY

Eph. 6:1–17; 1 Pet. 1:24–25; Heb. 4:12

1. How does Paul describe the Word of God?

2. What does it have the ability to do?

Jesus used the written Scriptures of the Old Testament in many of His addresses to the people, but I think that what Mark is telling us here is that it was the 'word' in the midst of the multiplicity of words. When people heard His words, they recognised that there was something else present; something that could only be explained as the authentic 'word' in the midst of words. Perhaps an illustration will help. Most people have heard of the famous Gettysburg address given by Abraham Lincoln. Not everyone realises, however, that a great orator spoke prior to Lincoln, and although his words were powerful and well chosen, what he had to say has been forgotten. In the multiplicity of words, there was no authentic 'word'. But afterwards, when Abraham Lincoln spoke simply and directly to the people, his listeners recognised in that brief speech the authenticity of the speaker. Thus, his speech is deathless.

How wonderful it would be if, when we speak, others would hear in the multiplicity of our words the 'word' of truth, the 'word' of heaven. No affectation, no unreality, no insincerity. Just that authentic 'word' coming through our words.

Yes, dear Father, help me use words in such a way that I get beyond them and bring that authentic 'word' to men and women – the 'Word made flesh'. In Jesus' name I ask it. Amen.

Speech that is simple

FOR READING & MEDITATION – MATTHEW 26:57–66; 27:11–14

'Tell us if you are the Christ, the Son of God.' (26:63)

The more we put Jesus' words and language under the spiritual microscope, the more we see how He demonstrated the art of reducing speech to simplicity. I heard a politician once say of another: 'Words were given to us to communicate our meaning, but the member opposite seems to have found another use for them.' Such an accusation could never be laid at Jesus. He was always simple, direct and to the point. There was great profundity, of course, in His parables, but when it was necessary for people to see His meaning right away, He put things to them in words that were perfectly clear.

In our reading today, we see Him standing before two different groups. Both asked Him different questions, but He did not answer them. However, when each group came to the crucial question and it was imperative that a clear reply be given, His answer was straightforward and unequivocal. He remained silent before the high priest's first question, yet when He was asked directly whether or not He was the Son of God, His reply was clear as crystal: 'Yes, it is as you say' (26:64). Later, when asked by Pilate the question, 'Are you the king of the Jews?' Jesus again replied: 'Yes, it is as you say' (27:11–12). Later still, however, when accused by the chief priests and elders, He made no reply. When a relevant issue arose He was simple and direct. When an irrelevant issue arose He maintained a majestic silence.

Ought we not to learn from this? Often we get so bogged down in dealing with the irrelevant that we have no time or energy to give to the relevant. We need to catch the simplicity and directness of our Master.

FURTHER STUDY

Isa. 53:1–7; Luke 23:9; Eccl. 3:7

1. How was prophecy fulfilled?

2. How did Jesus respond to Herod's questions?

Lord God, I long to be like Jesus in thought, word and deed. May this simplicity and directness of His, which has been occupying our thoughts over the past few days, become part of me also. In His name I pray. Amen.

Surrendered speech!

FOR READING & MEDITATION – COLOSSIANS 4:1–15

'Let your conversation be always full of grace, seasoned with salt' (v6)

If the world followed the way of Jesus, how much simpler things would be. I read recently that it was the Quakers who introduced the one price system in Europe in an effort to follow Jesus' instructions to let your 'Yes' be 'Yes' and your 'No' be 'No'. The writer pointed out that the abandonment of the bargaining system, which was prevalent in Europe (as it is now in many parts of the world), saved civilisation a good deal of bad temper and a whole lot of time. Millions of pounds and dollars are lost, not to say endless hours and days, because people don't know where they stand. In the light of what we have been seeing over these past few days – the simple, direct, and straightforward way in which Jesus communicated with the men and women of His day – how should we as His modern-day disciples live?

FURTHER STUDY

Titus 2:7–8; 2 Pet. 2:17–22; Col. 4:6

1. What was Paul's advice to Titus?

2. What should our conversation be like?

We need to reflect on how we communicate and relate to others and decide to bring our speech and our language in line with God's design. Inevitably, we need to surrender our speech to God for sifting. For some it may mean cutting out all affectation, all unreality, all insincerity, all weasel words, all talking for effect, all complicated and convoluted statements. As Christians, everything about us ought to ring true, especially our speech. We must try to avoid all loose statements about people, refuse to stick labels on them, and make sure that our words are a revelation, not of fantasy, but of truth.

I've heard it said: 'Words are the sounds of the heart.' Let's make it our aim to ensure that our heart and our words have the same sound – the sound of simplicity and love. When we are fundamentally simple, we are fundamentally sound.

My Father and my God, help me to be like a weaned child, weaned from all that complicates and all that is out of harmony with the Spirit of Your Son. This I ask in His precious and peerless name. Amen.

CWR Today

National Prayer Weekend

Your street, **your** community, **your** prayers

The National Prayer Weekend is an opportunity to make God's love known to those around you. Local people praying for their community can and does change lives.

'First of all, then, I urge that supplications, prayers, intercessions, and thanksgivings be made for all people'
(1 Tim. 2:1, ESV)

The idea is simple: ask people in your local area whether they would like prayer, then gather prayer requests together and pray for them during the National Prayer Weekend.

'The initiative opened the door for some very natural opportunities to share our testimonies with people both known and unknown to us.' (National Prayer Weekend 2016 participant church)

'Prayer matters, and prayer changes everything. Because as God changes us in prayer, He drives us out to be justice-seekers, peacemakers, healers and bringers of good news' (Justin Welby, the Archbishop of Canterbury, in response to the initiative)

Join in over the weekend of **29 September – 1 October 2017** by praying for your community. For more information, visit **www.national-prayer-weekend.com**

Vocabulary adjustment

FOR READING & MEDITATION – TITUS 2:1–15

'In your teaching show... soundness of speech that cannot be condemned' (vv7–8)

We spend one last day meditating on the need to infuse our speech with simplicity.

The famous French philosopher, writer and historian Voltaire is reported to have said: 'The adjective is the enemy of the noun.' As someone who works with words, I have put down my New Testament many times when reading the sayings of Jesus and sat back enthralled at the way He put words together. His adjectives were not enemies of nouns but supporters of them. C.S. Lewis is a classic example of such a wordsmith. He once said he would no more use ornate language than ornate clothing.

The principal of the college I attended told the students in his farewell address: 'Regularly go over your vocabularies to see if you are using words out of which the content has dropped. The new generation of young people you face can sniff out all unreality – and sniff it from afar.' I discovered the truth of those words in one of the early churches I pastored. Whenever I stood up to teach, a young man in the congregation would take a book out of his pocket and begin to read. When I asked him why he did that he said: 'You're not being real. You are using words to impress, not teach.' I was devastated – devastated but disciplined. By the time I left that church the young man I mentioned had become one of my closest friends. His challenge helped me become a better teacher and pastor.

If we, as Jesus' twenty-first-century disciples, speak in such a way to people that they hear only words, then can we blame them if they too take out a book and read it?

FURTHER STUDY

1 Cor. 5:8; 2 Cor. 1:12–14; 2:17; 1 John 3:18

1. What was Paul's boast?

2. What made Paul different from 'so many'?

Father, Your Word says that by our words we shall be justified and by our words we shall be condemned. In the light of this I ask You to simplify my vocabulary. Remove from it all unreality and all veneer. In Jesus' name. Amen.

Simple – but not easy

FOR READING & MEDITATION – MATTHEW 18:1–9

'unless you change and become like little children, you will never enter the kingdom of heaven.' (v3)

After seeing how Jesus spoke with simplicity, we now look at the way He made the big issue of how we enter the kingdom of God one of simplicity. Today's text becomes our starting point for this brief journey. J.B. Phillips translates it: 'unless you change your whole outlook and become like little children you will never enter the kingdom of Heaven.' In other words, unless you come in the simplicity of childlike faith you cannot get in.

The essential difference between the Christian faith and every other religion is its simplicity. To find God, it says, you move away from all the complicated efforts of relying on my own performance to simple faith in God's Word. Picture a little child opening up a hand to receive a costly gift. See the delight on its face, the sense of eager anticipation, the joy that breaks out as the hand closes on the precious object. Can anything be simpler than that?

We should remember, however, that the entrance into the kingdom of God has been made simple is not the same as saying it is easy. For some, the very simplicity can put them off. A university professor who heard me speak at a meeting for businessmen in the City of London on today's passage dismissed much of what I said. He told a friend of mine after the meeting: 'The ideas the speaker presented were not demanding enough, not strenuous enough. He made the way into the kingdom of God too easy.' He missed the text entirely. I had not claimed it was easy – just simple. And it was not me who said that anyone who will not receive the kingdom of God like a little child will not enter into it, but Jesus.

FURTHER STUDY

Psa. 131:1–3; Mark 10:15; Luke 18:16

1. What is the psalmist's approach to God?

2. What condition did Jesus give for entrance to God's kingdom?

Lord God, how I long for my life to be full of simple, uncomplicated trust. Teach me in my relationship with You to become less and less complicated and more and more like a little child. In Jesus' name I pray. Amen.

Being in control

FOR READING & MEDITATION – ROMANS 10:5–21

'if you confess with your mouth, "Jesus is Lord," and believe in your heart... you will be saved.' (v9)

We begin with a question: If entering into God's kingdom is so simple, why is it that so many stumble over the fact? I think the answer is that becoming childlike is one of the most difficult things for us to do. Generally speaking, a child characteristically is an accepting, believing, and trusting individual. Adults who have been knocked about a bit by the world (and perhaps by difficult early relationships) tend to develop strong defences that militate against trust. They are more cautious, more judicious, more wary.

Education, too, can make it more difficult for us to accept the simple conditions that Jesus lays down for entrance into His kingdom. One of the things that used to surprise me in the early days of my ministry was to hear highly intelligent and well educated people say as they were being led to Christ: 'Is it really that simple?' They expected to be faced with some complicated theory, or required to memorise a creed. So when they were told all they had to do was to stop trying to save themselves and let Christ save them, to become as trusting as little children, it almost blew their minds.

We would much prefer to do something to save ourselves than to adopt a trusting childlike attitude, because strenuous self-effort gives us a feeling of being in control (see Naaman in 2 Kings 5:13–14). The one thing above all others that our human nature detests is the feeling of not being in control. But this feeling of helplessness (the opposite of being in control) is precisely the condition required for entering into the kingdom of God. For some it is easier to struggle than to trust. Easier, but not productive.

FURTHER STUDY

Matt. 16:1–16; 10:32; 1 John 4:15; John 20:28

1. What was Peter's confession?

2. What was Thomas' confession?

Lord, I recognise that this desire to be in control is part of my fallen condition and leads me to want to be in control of the way in which I find salvation. Lead me to a childlike trust in You and Your Word. Amen.

'God has no grandchildren'

FOR READING & MEDITATION – JOHN 1:1–14

'born not of natural descent, nor of human decision or a husband's will, but born of God.' (v13)

The verse before us today is one of those classic New Testament verses that crystallises for us the truth we have been looking at over the past few days. Even though most of my readers, I know, are Christians, it will do us no harm to pause and focus on the truth of our salvation once again.

The passage highlights, among other things, that we cannot gain entrance into the kingdom of God by natural means, or, as the text puts it, by 'natural descent'. We can't expect to get into God's kingdom because our parents were Christians or because we were born in a Christian country. Being born in a Christian home may give you a push in the right direction, but you as a person have to decide and make a life commitment. As someone put it: 'God has no grandchildren.'

The second thing our text points out is that entrance into God's kingdom is not 'of human decision'. Other translations say this: 'not of the will of the flesh'. It means you don't get in by whipping up the will, striving a little harder, being more faithful in religious exercises, and so on. Entrance comes, not by stirring up our will but by surrender of our will.

Third, it does not come through the will of man or, as our text puts it: 'a husband's will'. No person can get you into the kingdom – no pastor, no priest. The prerogative is God's, and God's alone. The only way in is by simplicity of spirit: 'Yet to all who received him... he gave the right to become children of God' (v12). It all hinges on the receiving. You don't find God by climbing up the ladder of self-effort, to find Him on the topmost rung. You find Him at the bottom of the ladder, where He came down to us through His incarnation.

FURTHER STUDY

Acts 10:34–48; Rom. 8:15

1. What was the heart of Peter's message?

2. What was the result?

Heavenly Father, as I reflect on the gospel once again, it all seems so amazingly simple. Help me not to complicate it by my self-centred striving. I surrender to You now. Save me. In Jesus' name. Amen.

Here for the taking!

FOR READING & MEDITATION – DEUTERONOMY 30:11–20

'the word is very near you; it is in your mouth and in your heart' (v14)

If you contrasted all the great religions of the world with the Christian faith, what would you find? There would be many differences, of course, but one thing that would probably strike you most forcibly is the fact that whereas all the other religions are so complicated, the Christian faith is sublimely simple.

No other religion has a God who came down to earth to die for those who want to know Him. Theologians describe the coming of the Son of God to earth and becoming a human being as 'the incarnation'. And the meaning of the incarnation is simply that we do not have to ascend to heaven to attain union with God – God has come down to our level in order to attain union with us. As Alan Watts puts it in his book *Behold the Spirit* (no longer in print): 'Man does not have to climb to the infinite and become God, because, out of love, the infinite God descends to the finite and becomes man... Once we realise the futility of our pride, that we can neither ascend to God, nor by reasons of pride, prevent his descent to us, the proud core of egoism is dissolved.'

Other religions claim and often demand that we have to strive to find God. Christianity says the very opposite – you simply have to let God find you. In other words, stay where you are, don't struggle, simply call out to God that you want Him to save you. As has often been said: 'Religions are man's search for God; Christianity is God's search for man.' That is why there are many religions, but only one gospel. The kingdom of God is as close as your next breath. If you reach out to try and earn it, you reach too far. It is here. And here for the taking!

FURTHER STUDY

Phil. 2:1–11; Rom. 8:3; 1 John 4:2

1. How does Paul describe the incarnation to the Philippians?

2. How does Paul compare the incarnation to the law?

Father, You bring all this so close that I am almost overwhelmed. Help me see that salvation comes not through my own striving but through simply receiving. Amen.

'To live like Mr Murray'

FOR READING & MEDITATION – GALATIANS 1:11–24

'to reveal his Son in me' (v16)

Before we leave the subject of how Jesus simplifies the big issue of entry to His kingdom, there is one more facet I would like to mention. Christians need not complicate what Christ has made simple. Sometimes we overlay the simple invitation of Jesus with creeds, ceremonies, ordinances, and rituals that put many off. Creeds do have their place in providing precision to elements of faith and preventing error, but their place is behind Christ, not in front of Him.

I heard of a rather self-important bishop in India who asked some confirmation candidates: 'What does it mean to be a Christian?' He expected an involved and complicated theological answer, so imagine his surprise when one of the group said: 'To live like Mr Murray.' Mr Murray was the missionary who had taught them. Their definition of Christianity might be thought by some to be too simple. But was it? I don't think so. They had caught the heart of Christianity – to reflect the nature and character of Jesus.

It would be wrong of me to suggest that there are no complicated issues in Christianity. There are still many theological knots I have not yet untied – even after many decades of studying the Scriptures. But the basics are simple. It is a matter of trusting Jesus. Complicated creeds and systems give way to the uncomplicated. Yes, as a person grows as a Christian then it is to be expected that their understanding of the faith will grow (1 Cor. 14:20) but the only way to enter the kingdom is to give your trust to Jesus in the same way that a child trusts a loving parent. The Christian life begins with simplicity of spirit. And if it doesn't begin there – it just doesn't begin.

FURTHER STUDY

Col. 1:1–27; 1 Cor. 11:1; 2 Thess. 3:9; Phil. 3:17

1. What is the hope of glory?

2. What was Paul able to say?

Gracious and loving heavenly Father, forgive us for the way in which we sometimes complicate Your truth by our desire to be profound. Help us see that great issues are always simple. In Jesus' name. Amen.

'The Father's style'

FOR READING & MEDITATION – MATTHEW 11:20–30

'you have hidden these things from the wise and learned, and revealed them to little children.' (v25)

Everything about Jesus was and is fundamentally simple and uncomplicated. We have seen how He brought lucidity to speech, how He simplified the big issue of how we enter the kingdom of God, and now we focus on His longing for this same simplicity to be characteristic of His followers also.

We see from our text today that once we are in the kingdom nothing is revealed except to the simple-hearted. Here revelation, or the unfolding of His purposes, is reduced to simplicity. Note that I use the words 'simple-hearted', not 'simple-minded', for as you know, the difference between those words is the difference of two worlds. The Amplified Bible (Classic Edition) puts today's text in these words: 'You have hidden these things from the wise and clever and learned, and revealed them to babies [to the childish, untaught, and unskilled]. Yes, Father... such was Your gracious will and good pleasure.' Look again at the words: 'Your gracious will and good pleasure.' It is the chosen purpose of God to reveal things to the simple-hearted. He chooses to do so because He delights to do so. As someone once put it: 'It is the Father's style.'

FURTHER STUDY

Isa. 55:6–11; Eph. 1:18; Rom. 10:10

1. Why do we need to put our natural thinking to one side?

2. What did Paul pray might be enlightened?

The precondition for seeing and understanding the things of God is simple-heartedness – a willingness to lay aside our own thinking so that we might absorb His. I have mentioned before a great educationalist who said: 'The first step in education is the admission of how much you do not know.' This is the first step in the kingdom of God also. It might unsettle those who like to feel they are always in control, but the truth is this – in the kingdom the simple-hearted see and know; the rest are blind.

Father, while I do not want to be simple-minded, I do want to be simple-hearted. Help me to admit how much I do not know so that I can become an eager candidate in the school of the Spirit. In Jesus' name I pray. Amen.

Two kingdoms – one law

FOR READING & MEDITATION – MATTHEW 5:1–12

'Blessed are the poor in spirit, for theirs is the kingdom of heaven.' (v3)

After hearing me speak on the subject of surrender of the heart and mind being the key to understanding the things of God, a nuclear scientist said: 'I believe that is equally true in the realm of nature as it is in the realm of grace.' I asked him to explain what he meant and this was his reply: 'If I stand before the door of the universe in a demanding mood and insist on knowing what is going on, the secrets of the universe will be largely unknown to me. If, however, I sit as a humble questioner, the door opens and I see far more than I would otherwise.' I repeated this statement to another scientist (also a Christian) and he said: 'The man is too passive. I have had to strive and struggle for all the knowledge I have gained.' Sadly in his drivenness, I fear he missed the point.

Of course an effort has to be made to study and research, but the true unfolding comes only through surrender. To learn we must first listen. And if we won't listen then we won't learn. I have come to agree with my scientist friend's comment that surrender of heart and mind is as true in the realm of nature as it is in the realm of grace. A question I often put to scientists was this: 'Are the discoveries of science mainly the result of an aggressive spirit or a humble spirit?' Nine times out of ten the answer is: 'A humble spirit.' The scientist who has no humility will discover the secrets of the universe but the scientist who sits quietly before the universe in an attitude of surrender will discover those secrets more readily. The same principle applies in the kingdom of grace.

FURTHER STUDY

Matt. 18:1–4; Prov. 22:4; James 4:10; 1 Tim. 1:15

1. What did Jesus say about humility of heart?

2. How did Paul show humility of heart?

Dear Lord, thank You for showing me this truth, that just as the kingdom of nature yields its precious secrets to those who are humble-minded, so it is also in the kingdom of grace. May I too have this humble spirit. In Jesus' name. Amen.

An open secret

FOR READING & MEDITATION – MATTHEW 13:1–17

'The knowledge of the secrets of the kingdom of heaven has been given to you, but not to them.' (v11)

We saw yesterday that the secrets of both the kingdom of nature and the kingdom of grace are revealed to those who have a humble spirit, not an aggressive, driven spirit. In today's verse, Jesus speaks of the secrets of the kingdom of heaven being given to those who have eyes to see and ears to hear.

Moffatt's translation of our text for today quite intrigues me, and reads like this: 'It is granted you to understand the open secrets of the Realm of heaven.' God has built into His universe both in the realm of nature and of grace some wonderful and precious secrets, but it must be remembered they are 'open secrets' that are uncovered more by humility of mind than an aggressive search. Though some effort of thought is needed of course (please don't hear me minimising that), much more depends on our attitude than the workings of the mind. Electricity was in the universe from the time of creation, but not until Benjamin Franklin conducted his experiments was its potential to be harnessed realised. The possibility of being heard around the world was there from the beginning, but it was Marconi who detected it. If you read the biographies of great inventors and discoverers, men like Franklin, Marconi, Newton, and so on, you will find one thing common to them all – a keen mind and a humble spirit.

'The secret of discovering things,' someone said, 'is a spirit – a spirit of self-surrendered humility.' The first step is to be humble, to be teachable, to cease struggling, stop fighting – and listen. Someone is speaking – and speaking authoritatively.

FURTHER STUDY

2 Sam. 7:1–19; 1 Kings 3:1–7; Matt. 3:14

1. How did David show humility of heart?
2. How did John the Baptist display humility?

Gracious Father, I see that, just as in life, the first lesson I learn when I come into Your kingdom is to listen. Sharpen my mind, my capacity to think, but above all – sharpen my ability to listen to Your voice. In Jesus' name. Amen.

Heart-first into life

FOR READING & MEDITATION – MATTHEW 21:1–11

'See, your king comes to you, gentle and riding on a donkey' (v5)

We have been seeing that Jesus made clear that understanding the things that relate to the kingdom of God are not given to those who rely upon their own brilliance but to those with humility. I am not being anti-intellectual when I say that, but simply recognising a law which God has set in the universe and which non-Christians sometimes see and, to some degree at least, understand.

Someone, who to the best of my knowledge was not a Christian, wrote in a magazine article: 'We must not try to manipulate life; rather we must try to find out what life demands of us, and train ourselves to fulfil these demands. It is a long and humble business.' Note that last phrase: 'It is a long and *humble* business' (emphasis mine). Those who demand of life instead of listening to what life demands of them end up tired, disconsolate, and dispirited. The results are written in frustration and wreckage. Does life say to us: If you won't be humble then you will be humbled? It would seem so. H.G. Wells declared that the psychologist can stand alongside the preacher and say that unless you are free from all preoccupation with self-interest there is a disintegration of the personality.

Both Phyllis Bottome and H.G. Wells are saying what Jesus said but in different words, namely that the path to growth, development, and knowing involves a freedom from arrogance, self-interest and self-centredness. In other words – simple-heartedness. The world tends to applaud those who go into life head-first – with the right kind of intellect. God applauds those who go into life heart-first – with the right kind of attitude.

FURTHER STUDY

Matt. 5:1–15; Gal. 5:22–23; James 1:21; Eph. 4:2

1. What is the result of a meek and humble spirit?

2. How are we to accept the Word?

Father, I understand that You are not against intellect – indeed You designed it – but You long above everything that I might have the right attitude of my heart – the attitude of Jesus. Amen.

'A pop-up of surprises'

FOR READING & MEDITATION – 1 CORINTHIANS 2:1–16

'the things that come from the Spirit of God... are spiritually discerned.' (v14)

Our thoughts have been engaged over the past few days with the idea that in God's kingdom nothing is revealed except to the simple-hearted. To understand, and to know what God wants us to know, requires not so much a keen or clever mind, but a childlike and humble spirit. That takes the pressure off us as it means the secrets of the kingdom are not given only to those who are theologically erudite and astute, but to ordinary people like you or me.

An acquaintance of mine, a man with a brilliant mind and a PhD in theology, told me that although he had earned a degree in theology, he was not really a Christian. He came into the ministry, pastored a church for several years, but did not know Christ in a personal way. One night an evangelist preached at his church, and the minister realised that although he knew much about the Bible, he did not know Jesus in the way the evangelist was presenting Him. So in his own church, and in front of all the people, he left the pulpit, knelt at the front, and took Christ as his personal Saviour. He said that immediately the Bible became a new book. He saw things he had never seen before. It was, as he put it, 'a pop-up of surprises'.

FURTHER STUDY

Psa. 119:49–60; Rom. 8:6; Phil. 4:8; Isa. 26:3

1. What wise decision did the psalmist take?

2. What brings life and peace?

Our text for today makes clear that while we can apply our best reasoning to the Bible (in the same way that we would apply it to any other body of literature), we can never fully grasp the Bible's treasures by intellect alone. I'm so glad that to understand 'spiritual truths' we do not need to have the wisdom of this world, but rather they are accessible to all who have a simple and humble spirit – to those who are open to God.

Father, I am thankful that though You do not bypass the intellect, You do not depend upon it to reveal Your truth to me. Providing my spirit is right, my lack of cleverness is not a barrier to You. Blessed be Your name forever. Amen.

Your help **has changed lives**

'One person gives freely, yet gains even more' (Prov. 11:24)

God's generosity can defy our logic. Selwyn Hughes refers to this as 'divine mathematics' in his book *Service in the Eighth Degree*: 'How can one little jar of flour and one small jug of oil be used to supply the needs of a widow for weeks and weeks and weeks? It doesn't make sense.'

At CWR, we owe our thanks to the divine mathematics of God and to the generosity of our Partners and supporters. Recent giving has aided the development of a daily Bible reading app for young adults, and will send thousands of copies of *40 Stories of Hope* into prisons in the UK. Thank you for your gifts that help us send biblical resources to those calling out to know more about God. Thank you for your donations that enable us every year to teach thousands of people about counselling and helping others.

We look forward with anticipation for what we will see accomplished next, through your generous giving.

If you would like to give to our current appeal, fill in the 'Gift to CWR' section on the order form at the back of these notes, completing the Gift Aid declaration if appropriate, or visit **www.cwr.org.uk/donate**. Thank you.

Two ways to be rich

FOR READING & MEDITATION – LUKE 12:13–21

'a man's life does not consist in the abundance of his possessions.' (v15)

We move on now to explore another aspect of the way in which Jesus addresses living more simply, and we focus on His words that life is not to be found in the possession of things, but in being rich towards God. This, of course, cuts clean across the mood of the many, for the majority believe that the more they own the greater their chance of having a happy and fulfilled life. Jesus clearly contradicts this way of thinking, and in so doing distils life to the simple and the vital.

Somewhere I read that you can be rich in two ways: in the abundance of your possessions or the fewness of your wants. When you are content with what you have, then you will learn to be rich. I love the story of the missionary who welcomed a newcomer to the mission station with these words: 'Make a list of all the things you think you need and I will show you how to get along without them.' However, let me be clear, Jesus does not say and is not saying it is wrong to possess things (providing those things have been acquired fairly and honestly), but that life is not to be found in possessions.

A bishop of the Early Church who had very little of this world's goods but was a remarkable example of the virtue of contentment was asked his secret. The venerable old man replied: 'It consists in nothing more than making a right use of my eyes. I first look up to heaven and remember my principal business is to get there. Then I look down to the earth and call to mind how small a place I shall occupy when I die and am buried. This enables me to keep a right perspective.' Some might say his philosophy was not simple but simplistic. I say it was simplicity sublime.

FURTHER STUDY

Eccl. 2:17–23; Matt. 6:19–20; 1 Tim. 6:7

1. What conclusion did the writer of Ecclesiastes come to?

2. What did Jesus teach about treasures?

Gracious and loving heavenly Father, help me lay hold of this truth that whatever I do or do not possess, when I possess You, then I am truly rich. Help me want more of You and less of things. In Jesus' name. Amen.

40 acres for free!

FOR READING & MEDITATION – PHILIPPIANS 4:10–20

'I have learned the secret of being content in any and every situation' (v12)

We ended yesterday with the story of the bishop who had very little of this world's goods but was a remarkable example of the virtue of contentment. He had learned from Jesus how to put things in the right perspective.

We live in a world that is harmfully preoccupied with possessions and material wealth. Survey after survey reveal that people equate happiness and contentment with their physical circumstances, and many grapple with anxiety and stress in their strenuous efforts to fill the emptiness that lies deep within. They say: 'If you have a nice home, a happy marriage, an adequate income, a wide circle of dependable friends, congenial work and good health, you can be happy. Without these things, you cannot.' But life does not conform to this equation. People who have all the things that others say are necessary to happiness often lack any joy. Some of the most discontented people in the world are those who have everything life can offer. True contentment is found in the right inner attitude, not in material possessions.

A favourite story of mine is of an old Quaker who advertised that he would give 40 acres of rich farmland to anyone who could prove that he was perfectly satisfied with what he had. A long line of men and women gathered outside his house, far too many for him to interview individually. So the old Quaker stood on his doorstep and said: 'All thou who art perfectly satisfied with what thou hast, raise thy hands.' Everybody raised their hands. 'Then why dost thou want this land?' asked the Quaker. The crowd looked at each other in silence and, seeing his point, one by one they shuffled away.

FURTHER STUDY

Luke 3:1–14; Prov. 15:16; 1 Tim. 6:6; Heb. 13:5

1. What did John exhort the soldiers to do?

2. What did Paul say was great gain?

Lord Jesus Christ, You who simplified everything, please teach me that selfsame simplicity. Give me the mind that was in You, then I too shall be simple and straightforward. For Your own dear name's sake. Amen.

Stewards, not proprietors

FOR READING & MEDITATION – PROVERBS 19:20–29

'The fear of the LORD leads to life: Then one rests content, untouched by trouble.' (v23)

The age in which we live is so caught up in the pursuit of possessions, that as followers of Jesus we need to seriously ask ourselves whether we have caught that same spirit too. It is all too easy for us to be caught up and swept along in the prevailing world-view and, without realising it, to have the world's false and unrealistic value systems influence and even direct our lifestyles.

However, I do not share the view some Christians propagate that believers ought to follow Jesus in renouncing all material possessions. I do not think that is what the Scripture is talking about when it encourages us to adopt the simplicity that is in Christ. We strike a balanced note in all this. God is not against us possessing things, but He is against them possessing us. It may be right for some Christians to give up their material possessions. For example, C.T. Studd, the famous missionary, gave away his inheritance to become a servant of Christ on foreign fields. But God does not require that of everybody. Other Christians may find God endowing them with material possessions because He wants them to be stewards of those things and use the resources for the advancement of His kingdom.

The 'simplicity that is in Christ', as it relates to possessions, is first and foremost a philosophy, a mindset. It is a mindset that says although I may own certain things, I will not be owned by them. I will live my life in such a way that though I be stripped of these things, it will in no way affect the peace that resides within my heart. When you can live independently of things then you are rich indeed.

FURTHER STUDY

Matt. 19:16–23; Luke 19:8; Acts 2:44–45

1. Why did Jesus require the young man to dispose of his possessions?

2. How did Zacchaeus respond to his salvation?

Lord, how complicated life is when we have many material things to secure and protect. Help me to see that whatever I have has come from You, and that I am the steward, not the proprietor. In Jesus' name I ask it. Amen.

Discontent!

FOR READING & MEDITATION – MATTHEW 5:21–30

'And if your right hand causes you to sin, cut it off and throw it away.' (v30)

How simple life would be if we would only follow Jesus' words and see that life consists not in the abundance of our possessions but in the richness of our relationship with God. The more our hearts become entwined around material things, the more unhappy we will be. Jesus knew the deep waters into which people would fall when they allowed themselves, for whatever reason, to be drawn away from God. Hence the extremely graphic words in today's passage – words that should not be too quickly set aside, but taken to heart.

I once saw a cartoon that depicted two fields divided by a fence. Both fields appeared to be about the same size, and each had plenty of the same kind of grass, green and lush. In each field was a mule, and each mule had its head through the fence, eating grass from the other mule's pasture. All around both mules was plenty of grass, yet the grass in the other field seemed greener or fresher, although it was harder to get. The cartoon depicted also that the mules, in their effort to eat the grass in the other's pasture, had got caught up in the fencing and were unable to extricate themselves. One word at the bottom of the cartoon summed it all up – 'Discontent'. It reminded me of what a comedian once said: 'If the grass looks greener on the other side of the fence, you can bet the water bill is much higher.' After all, the psalmist warns us not to be like a mule (Psa. 32:9)!

These words of Thomas à Kempis were given to me by a friend at my ordination service when I came into the ministry, and they are words that made a profound impression upon me at the time: 'Constantly choose rather to want less, than to have more.'

FURTHER STUDY

James 2:1–5;
Phil. 3:8;
1 Tim. 6:17–19

1. What has God called us to be rich in?

2. What is certain about the bank of heaven?

Father, drive the truths I am facing right now even more deeply into my spirit, and help me grasp the fact that I am rich in proportion to the number of things I can afford to leave alone. In Jesus' name. Amen.

'Giving way to the simple'

FOR READING & MEDITATION – 1 TIMOTHY 6:3–16

'But godliness with contentment is great gain.' (v6)

We spend one more day discussing how Jesus simplified life here on earth by revealing to us the complications that can arise in our hearts when we allow ourselves to become enamoured with 'stuff'.

Over the years I have talked to many people whose businesses have crashed, but I remember one in particular: a fine, spiritually-minded man who responded to my question as to how he was handling his new circumstances in this way: 'I think little about what I haven't and a lot about what I have.' 'Considering what you have gone through,' I asked him, 'how would you now define Christianity?' He thought for a moment and said: 'The complicated giving way to the simple.' I was amazed at his insight and came away conscious more of being helped than of having been a helper.

In the light of what we have been saying over these past few days, may I suggest that you go over your life and see if there are any complications in your outer life that are coming from your inner life. Are there, for example, mixed motives? Perhaps you say to yourself, 'Possessions and material things mean little or nothing to me,' yet subconsciously this may not be so. It is so easy for the subconscious to mislead the conscious and be at cross-purposes. But remember – all self-examination is best carried out in God's presence and, after prayer, inviting Him to search your heart. Then, in a calm frame of mind, discover what God can uncover. If it is clear there are complicated motives, then give them into the hands of God. This could be an important day for you – a day when you move away from inner complexity and complication to simplicity and sureness.

FURTHER STUDY

Psa. 139:17–24; Prov. 16:2; 1 Cor. 4:5

1. What will God bring to light?

2. Pray the prayer of the psalmist.

Lord God, search my heart as I wait in Your presence. Although I am in union with You, far too often I can be a nervous, anxious, and complicated person. Please make me more childlike – simple, uncomplicated and unafraid. Amen.

The way – for everything

FOR READING & MEDITATION – JOHN 14:1–14

'I am the way and the truth and the life.' (v6)

We move now to examine the important issue of how Jesus reduced life's most troublesome and perplexing personal problems to the realm of simplicity. When Jesus said, 'I am the way,' He of course meant He was the only way to God. However He also meant (so I believe) that the answer to all our personal problems, whether spiritual or psychological, lies in Him. When I say 'personal problems' I am thinking of those things that drive people into counselling – difficulties in relating, temper losses, inner turmoil, depression, obsessive or compulsive thoughts, high anxiety, fear of failure, and so on. Providing they do not have their roots in a physical deficiency, these issues can, albeit sometimes with help, be overcome by entering into a deep, rich and ongoing personal relationship with Jesus Christ.

Now I realise that last statement will, to some, sound hopelessly naive and dangerously simplistic. It might even cause new readers to say: 'The writer sounds like one of those simple-minded fanatics who believes Jesus is the answer for everything.' I have trained in theology and psychology, pastored six churches, and have had over forty years' experience as a counsellor. In all that time I have noticed, when dealing with people's personal problems, that although they were so complex that it sometimes took months, sometimes years to understand and comprehend them, the actual solution – the key that unlocked the difficulty – was always relatively simple.

'All great personal problems,' someone once said, 'are a reduction from complexity to simplicity.' How I wish he would have added – the simplicity of Jesus.

FURTHER STUDY

Col. 2:1–7; 3:1–4; Isa. 11:2

1. What is hidden in Christ?

2. What had Isaiah prophesied?

My Father and my God, I have found the way not to live; now let me find the way to live – and live abundantly. I may sense some deep challenges coming up. So hold me close. In Jesus' name I ask it. Amen.

How problems arise

FOR READING & MEDITATION – JOHN 10:1–10

'I have come that they may have life, and have it to the full.' (v10)

Yesterday we said that although people's problems can be extremely complex, sometimes needing many hours to unravel, the solution to those problems, the key that unlocks the difficulty, is often simple. I am reminded of a sign I saw on the desk of a company director: 'The problem when solved will be simple.' Is this really so? If my experience is anything to go by, the answer is almost certainly 'Yes'.

Let's first consider how problems arise in the personality. There are, I believe, two main causes of personal problems – physical and spiritual. As a result of Adam and Eve's original sin in the Garden of Eden, we live in a fallen world where our bodies do not function in the way in which they were designed. And this physical malfunction can have a direct influence on our emotions, our attitudes and our outlook on life. This is why my advice to people who are struggling with serious emotional problems is to first have a thorough medical check-up to ensure that the problem is not a physiological malfunction.

Spiritual problems (and I include in that phrase what people call 'psychological' problems) are also a consequence of living in a fallen world. Every one of us was designed to live in a close and rich relationship with God, and when we don't then problems arise that sometimes get beyond our control. I am not attempting to persuade you to swallow naive ideas or to ignore real complexities when I say this, but I believe with all my heart that a rich relationship with God is the key to overcoming every personal problem there is. But believe me, to hold to that conviction without falling into shallowness or irrelevance is not easy.

FURTHER STUDY

Eph. 3:14–21; 2 Sam. 22:37; 2 Pet. 1:5–6

1. What did Paul pray for the Ephesians?

2. What are we to make every effort to do?

Father, I know that Your Son is the answer to my every need, but entering into the fullness of that experientially is something I can't always do. Help me, dear Father. In the Saviour's peerless and precious name. Amen.

'Trust and obey'

FOR READING & MEDITATION – 1 PETER 2:1–12

'the one who trusts in him will never be put to shame.' (v6)

Can what we are saying really be true? Does a deep, rich and ongoing relationship with God give us the empowerment we need to rise above all our personal problems and overcome them? What about such problems as depression, for example – depression not based on physical deficiencies, that is.

Time and time again I have seen depressions lift when people grasped in a fresh and clear way the reality of God's purpose for their lives and entered into it with abandonment and joy. And what about the prevailing endemic of anxiety and panic attacks? When we come to understand that God holds the future, and learn to take His promises more personally, something more powerful can take place than a mere therapeutic excursion into past traumas and childhood experiences. Not that journeys into the past aren't sometimes necessary and helpful (if only to understand where the problems began). But though the roots of many problems lie in the past, the solution is nearly always in the present – confident trust in God. Two lines of an old hymn I learned in Sunday school put it most clearly: 'Trust and obey, for there's no other way to be happy in Jesus but to trust and obey.'

Can it really be as simple as the old hymn suggests? The answer is 'Yes'. However, to take that simple truth and pass it on to someone in the same way that a doctor gives out a prescription, without taking the time (sometimes a long time) to build a bridge of empathy and understanding, can be reckless. We must remember it's not just the application of truth that heals, it's the manner in which that truth is given that helps to bring resolution to a person's problem.

FURTHER STUDY

Prov. 3:1–12; Psa. 32:10

1. What brings health and nourishment?

2. What surrounds the man who trusts in God?

Lord God, save me from the insensitivity that barges into the lives of those who are in the midst of deep personal problems and says, 'Just trust Jesus'. Help me see that I have to give myself to people before I give my words to them. Amen.

Psychology – or Christ?

FOR READING & MEDITATION – JEREMIAH 6:9–16

'Stand at the crossroads and look; ask for the ancient paths' (v16)

If there is a 'simplicity in Christ' that applies to the matter of personal problems, I fear it may have eluded many Christian counsellors of our day. It is a matter of deep concern when churches take on board ideas concerning the art of helping people with their problems that leave out Christ and sometimes even contravene His teaching. How can we hope to resolve people's problems when we bypass Christ and the Scriptures, where the best resources for people-helping are to be found?

The danger facing Christian counselling as it stands at the crossroads of different ways of helping people is that of turning to psychological theories that leave out Christ. Many (thank God not all) are attracted to solutions that substitute fascinating ideas for reality, and interesting humanistic theories for the tried and tested truths of Scripture. I am not against people studying the subject of psychology (I have studied the subject widely myself) but, ultimately, that is not what is going to help people when they are caught up in the throes of inner conflict. Something is wrong when we in the Church turn from the way of simplicity to theories that have no compatibility with Scripture and originate from a secular world-view.

FURTHER STUDY

Heb. 12:1–13; Psa. 16:1–11; 119:35; Prov. 4:18

1. What was David's testimony?

2. What results when we choose the right path?

Jeremiah was disappointed with the leaders of his day who applied the wrong remedies to people's problems. What would he say, I wonder, if he were alive today? Probably the same thing, only with much more emphasis and concern. If the Christian community isn't able to clearly articulate its God-given gift to people-helping and the instilling of the peace of God's presence and lasting hope in the world, I fear for the next generations.

Lord God my Father, forgive us as Your people that we so often resort to the world for ideas, when You have given us such endless resources in Christ. Help us to put the emphasis where You always put it – on Jesus. In His name I pray. Amen.

The National Prayer Weekend 2017 begins today! If you haven't already, visit www.national-prayer-weekend.com

Make space in your life to connect with God, learn new skills and explore your faith.

Introduction to Biblical Care and Counselling

This renowned five-day course is for anyone who wants to learn more about themselves and how to help others effectively. It is also ideal for those involved in pastoral care or thinking about counselling training, whatever their level of experience.
The next course is 13–17 November.

'A brilliant week – a place to dip your toe in to counselling in a very safe environment.'

Woman to Woman

Spend five days on this inspiring course, designed for women of all ages who want to encourage and minister to other women. It is brimming with opportunities for you to learn and grow as you understand more about yourself and explore your gifts, vision, spirituality and abilities.
The next course is 5–9 March 2018.

'It was such a significant week. I feel so much more settled about what my "calling" is.'

These courses have a residential or non-residential option. For more information, call **+44 (0)1252 784719** or visit **www.cwr.org.uk/courses**

SAT
30 SEP

A growth-stopper

FOR READING & MEDITATION – JUDGES 2:16–23

'They refused to give up their evil practices and stubborn ways.' (v19)

We have been saying that when it comes to the matter of personal problems – the kind that drive people into counselling – there is a 'simplicity in Christ' that is being missed by many in the Church. 'It is too simple and naive,' said someone to me once, 'to maintain that deep psychological problems can be resolved in a relationship with God. Other methods must be used also; science and Scripture must work hand in hand.' Others raise the question: What about those who do have an apparently good relationship with God but still struggle with troubles like depression, anorexia nervosa, anxiety, obsessive compulsive disorders, and so on?

What has amazed me as a veteran Christian is how I can maintain a fairly good relationship with God on the surface yet still depend deep down on my own resources for holding my life together. I know the answers to my problems, whether they be personal or otherwise, are to be found in Jesus – that is a simple and established biblical fact. But when you ask me to trust the invisible God to make my life work, rather than depending on the things I can see and I know have worked for me over the years, I am conscious that within me is a stubborn commitment to independence that is sometimes quite frightening.

Independence, I suspect, is the real problem that hinders our development as persons and the giving of ourselves in abandoned trust to Christ. When we are willing to deal with it, we shall discover that whatever relationship we had with God before is as nothing compared to that which flows out of a deep and fully dependent trust.

FURTHER STUDY

Judg. 17:1–6; 21:25; Prov. 14:12; 16:25

1. What is written of the period of Judges when Israel had no king?

2. What conclusion does the writer of Proverbs come to?

Father, however well I know You, help me know more of You. Help me see my stubbornness – the stubbornness that blames You for not coming to my aid when really I'm not willing to come to You. Forgive me, my Father. In Jesus' name. Amen.

30 years

after the *miracle* of Waverley Abbey House

God is still moving.

This September we honour God for answering the prayers of Selwyn Hughes 30 years ago by giving CWR a home. Even the lawyers assisting with the purchase of Waverley Abbey House saw the fingerprints of God all over it.

As co-founder Trevor J. Partridge said at the house's opening in 1987:

'It's no accident that this house lies in the shadow of Abbey ruins... that 12 monks in 1128 dedicated this whole parcel of land to the living God.'

In Scripture, dedication to a calling often began at 30 years of age; Aaronic priests were dedicated to serve at 30, and Jesus initiated His ministry aged 30. We have seen God growing the impact of His ministry through CWR, and for 30 years now Waverley Abbey House has been a place of teaching and inspiring God's people and developing His Church.

We believe that 30 years after God moved miraculously for CWR, He calls us, together, to continue to grow His work.

God has used Waverley Abbey House as a centre of calling and sending for 30 years. He has established a strong foundation from which CWR can increase its reach in serving the Church, the nation and the world.

Serving the Church

Just as Aaronic priests spent 30 years preparing for ministry, we believe God is preparing to increase the ministry of CWR. God has blessed our resources enabling us to reach over one million readers this year.

Serving the nation

The 184 UK students currently on our Higher Education programmes show God's love through Christian counselling and pastoral care to hundreds of people in churches, schools and communities.

Serving the world

God continues to work miracles as this year our Christian counselling and pastoral care courses are being taught in Cambodia and Singapore. CWR resources have been translated into eight different languages this year alone.

Why we do this? To help people live God's way, every day.
And CWR's ministry is only just beginning…

JOIN US AS THE JOURNEY CONTINUES

Help us serve the Church as we dedicate ourselves to reaching all generations with God's Word by developing new technologies and content, particularly to help young adults apply the Bible to their lives, every day.

Help us serve the nation as we honour God's invitation to prayer through initiatives such as the National Prayer Weekend, and continue our ministry of biblical teaching with courses, seminars and Higher Education programmes.

Help us serve the world by continuing our Christian counselling programmes in Singapore and Asia, and responding to the requests for translations and training in China and around the world.

Join us and become a CWR Partner as we respond to God's call to continue serving the Church, the nation and the world. Will you respond with us?

Our Partners enable all that we do by giving both prayer and financial support. They help us reach people who want to learn more about God's Word, sending tens of thousands of free copies of Bible reading notes into UK and Australian prisons, schools and libraries every year, and send valuable resources to church leaders in the developing world.

To make a donation to the work of CWR, turn to the back of this publication. To become a CWR Partner, see the next page.

CWR Partners

Becoming a CWR Partner, and making a regular donation to CWR, will enable us to plan new initiatives and continue to reach thousands of people with life-changing teaching and resources. You will also be invited to special events to hear more about our ministry and receive news updates.

Want to hear more? Contact **partners@cwr.org.uk**

To become a CWR Partner, complete the form below and return it to:
CWR Partnership, Waverley Abbey House, Waverley Lane, Farnham, Surrey GU9 8EP
or contact **partners@cwr.org.uk** for more information.

To (name of bank/building society): ____________________

Address (of bank/building society): ____________________

____

Please pay the account of CWR, account no. 20309079 at Barclays Bank PLC, 22 The Borough, Farnham, Surrey GU9 7NH (sort code 20-31-06) the sum of

(in words) ____________________ **pounds**

£ _____ **:** _____ **p (amount in figures), quoting:**

Surname: ____________________

Commencing on the _____ **day of** _____ **2017, and every month on the same day until otherwise notified.**

Name on account: ____________________

Account no.: ____________________

Signature of account holder: ____________________ **Date:** __________

Address: ____________________

____

____

Postcode: __________

I understand that my donation will be used for CWR ministry in the UK and overseas, wherever the need is greatest. The allocation of funds is the responsibility of the CWR Board of Directors.
I may increase or discontinue my regular gifts by notifying CWR. As a Partner, my opinions may be sought on programme issues but confers no legal rights beyond those of a donor.

Non-defensive living

FOR READING & MEDITATION – LUKE 12:1–12

'When you are brought before... authorities, do not worry... for the Holy Spirit will teach you' (vv11–12)

Another area of life that Jesus simplified so beautifully is that which relates to our personal identity – who we are as persons. If we are uncomfortable with ourselves and have no deep inner security, then we tend to become defensive in an attempt to prove to others that we are more secure than we actually are. Jesus, I believe, had no need of defences because He knew who He was and experienced a deep inner security that characterised everything He did and everything He said.

'Do not worry,' says Jesus, 'about how you will defend yourselves or what you will say,' when brought before the authorities to explain the basis of your faith. 'The Holy Spirit will teach you at that time what you should say.' Some Christians think these words of Jesus teach us that if we are involved in a court action we shouldn't defend ourselves. That is not what this scripture is saying. There is nothing wrong (in my opinion) in presenting an honest defence. Indeed, one has a clear responsibility to resist deceit, lies and dishonesty with the truth. Who would dare to suggest that the apostle Paul was being unscriptural when he laid out his defence before Agrippa in Acts 26?

The thought underlying the words of Jesus in our text today has more to do (so I believe) with what has been described as 'defensiveness'. Defensiveness is the attitude we develop when we are unsure of ourselves and, due to the anxiety this causes deep within, we relate to others from a position of weakness rather than strength. Life is always complicated for the defensive; they get all tied up within. But why be complicated when you can be simple? Life is so much better the Jesus way.

FURTHER STUDY

Acts 5:1–11; Prov. 23:7

1. What were Ananias and Sapphira looking to for their security?

2. What was at the heart of their actions?

Living Christ, give me Your mind, Your security, Your steadfastness. Then I too shall be simple and straightforward. I want a heart that loves the simple and the true. Give me that heart. For Your own dear name's sake. Amen.

That's trust!

FOR READING & MEDITATION – PSALM 62:1–12

'My soul finds rest in God alone; my salvation comes from him.' (v1)

Today we continue thinking through the issue of defensiveness. We are using this word because it better explains what Jesus was getting at in yesterday's passage. As we said, those who live in a constant state of defensiveness – because they are not really sure of themselves and of their resources – end up living complicated lives. Often they nervously try to explain things, and finish up overstating their case and making other people nervous. What Jesus is advocating is that we become the kind of people who are confident in and of God, so trusting of the Holy Spirit that we have no need of defensiveness. This means that we can defend ourselves whenever it is necessary, but not in a way that is defensive.

Confused? Then let me explain. Secure persons will, when called to explain their behaviour, do so in a clear, gentle, and loving way. But if the explanation is not accepted, they will feel no inner need or compulsion to remonstrate with an accuser and press their point until it becomes boringly repetitive. They can afford, as the well-known saying puts it, 'to wait for the days and months to speak against the hours'.

A fine Christian man I know, a leader of a church, was accused of something of which he was innocent. He explained the facts, but his explanation was not accepted and he was removed from the pulpit of that church. I wondered why he hadn't done more to protest his innocence. With assurance he said: 'Truth is on my side... the months will speak against the hours.' Within six months he was exonerated and went back to the pulpit. Now that's security, that's trust.

FURTHER STUDY

Psa. 46:10; 71:3; Prov. 14:26; 18:10

1. What was God's word to the psalmist?

2. Why did he declare he would not fear?

Lord God, I must ask myself today: Am I nervous, anxious and complicated? If so, help me to know the experience of the psalmist, who said: 'My soul finds rest in God alone.' In Jesus' name I pray. Amen.

Defensive projection

FOR READING & MEDITATION – 1 SAMUEL 19:1–10

'My father Saul is looking for a chance to kill you. Be on your guard' (v2)

Defensive people are often anxious people. And to cope with the anxiety they become more and more defensive. Thus life becomes more and more complicated. The story of King Saul illustrates how defensiveness can ruin relationships and paralyse potential.

King Saul had everything going for him – a striking appearance and he had been chosen as king. But out of the long list of characters in the Old Testament, I would choose Saul as being one of the most defensive of them all. His defensiveness can perhaps be traced back to his disobedience. From then on he was deeply insecure so it is not surprising that he used a device of the personality that is described in talking therapies as projection. This takes place when we attribute to someone else our own thoughts and feelings. We can't face these things in ourselves so we project them on to others and criticise them from a safe distance. Christians who react with deep anger and condemnation when they discover faults in others may well be exhibiting this type of defensiveness. I can't be entirely sure of this, but I often thought that Saul's desire to kill David, the young man who had arrived on the scene and who had won the hearts of all the people, arose because he persuaded himself that David wanted to get rid of him. If he did, then that would have been the device of projection at work.

When you read the story of King Saul in the first book of Samuel, you certainly get a picture of a man who, although he was called to be king, felt very insecure in his personality. His trust was largely in himself and not in God – a poor foundation on which to build a kingdom.

FURTHER STUDY

Psa. 118:1–8; 37:5;
Isa. 26:3–4

1. What conclusion had the psalmist come to?

2. What basis did Isaiah give for putting trust in God?

Father, help me see that defensive living is dangerous living. Show me how to put my trust in You so that deep down I might know a life free from inner complications. In Jesus' name I pray. Amen.

Secret sins

FOR READING & MEDITATION – 2 SAMUEL 12:1–13

'Then Nathan said to David, "You are the man!"' (v7)

Yesterday we had a little glimpse into King Saul's defensiveness, particularly as it related to his desire to kill David. Today we look at the same defensive device of projection in David himself who, you may remember, was described as 'a man after [God's] own heart' (1 Sam. 13:14).

Even God-fearing people can act defensively – and not know that they are doing it. David was so self-deceived in regard to his relationship with Bathsheba, and later the murder of Uriah, Bathsheba's husband, that his judgment became distorted. When Nathan came and presented to him his pointed parable, David overreacted and wanted the man in the story put to death. There were severe penalties for sheep-stealing in Israel, but never death (see Exod. 22:1). Because David had not dealt with the issues that had been going on in his own life, and had not repented of what without doubt are the most serious of sins – adultery and murder – he unconsciously projected his inner self-conflict onto someone else.

The thing we project onto other people, and dislike or try to control in them, is often the thing we are repressing in ourselves. In order to avoid personal discomfort we distort reality in ourselves and then try to get rid of our guilty feelings by transferring them onto others. In such moments it is not truth that controls us, but comfort. Such an attitude is dangerous to ourselves and others, and we must do everything we can to present ourselves regularly before the throne of grace and pray as David prayed in Psalm 139: 'Search me, O God, and know my heart... See if there is any offensive way in me, and lead me in the way everlasting' (vv23–24).

FURTHER STUDY

1 Chron. 28:9; Jer. 17:10; 23:24

1. What was David's advice to Solomon?
2. What did the Lord declare?

Lord God, I open every part of my life for Your inspection. Bring to the surface 'any offensive way in me', and cleanse me from every secret sin. This I ask in Christ's dear name. Amen.

The Word that is alive!

FOR READING & MEDITATION – HEBREWS 4:1–13

'For the word of God... penetrates even to dividing soul and spirit, joints and marrow' (v12)

Another aspect of defensiveness is denial. Forgive me for mentioning this issue once again (I am conscious I have written a good deal about it over the years), but the more I search my own heart and listen to the confessions of others, the more I see how denial, when present in our hearts, blocks the road to being an open and non-defensive personality.

Basically, denial is the refusal to admit to whatever is true. Actually, it is a way in which we attempt to dethrone God. When in denial we say to ourselves: 'God can't handle the real world so it must be changed in such a way that He can handle it.' A person who is not comfortable with reality has to construct a world that is untrue, but that, you see, is a denial of reality. The opposite of denial is integrity, or, if you prefer – non-defensiveness. The work of keeping reality at bay drains our energy – energy that properly would be directed into positive and productive living.

When I asked a group of students to give me a biblical illustration of denial, they all suggested Simon Peter. But his denial of Jesus (Luke 22:54–62) is not the kind of denial that I am talking about here. Peter's denial was a conscious one, the denial we are exploring is one we are not conscious of. Unless someone points it out to us, we remain unaware of what we are doing. The drive is unconscious and arises from those parts of us where the truth of God has not quite penetrated. That is why we take to heart the truth of today's verses, and allow the Word that is alive to evangelise not just a part, but to penetrate to the whole of our personalities.

FURTHER STUDY

Ezek. 37:1–10; Jer. 5:14; 23:29

1. What are some of the descriptions of God's Word?

2. How do these aspects impact the inner man?

Father God, evangelise my heart – all of it, not just part. Let the Word that is alive penetrate to the deep springs of my being so that even my unconscious is invaded by You. In Jesus' name I ask it. Amen.

One worth following

FOR READING & MEDITATION – JOHN 7:37–52

'No-one ever spoke the way this man does' (v46)

'Live defensively – buy a tank' was the caption of a cartoon I saw in a Christian counsellor's magazine. However, defensive living is not an option when it comes to following in the footsteps of the master. Comb the record of Jesus' life in the Gospels and you will not find one occasion when He was defensive. He spoke clearly about life's issues and chose the right words to convey His thoughts. But He was never drawn into protracted arguments and, having made His point, He never pressed it to the stage where He became argumentative. He was simple, unaffected and unafraid; the kind of person who could afford to 'wait for the days and months to speak against the hours'.

How different are our lives when compared to His – and how much more complicated! The most non-defensive man I have ever met was the principal of the Bible college I attended – John Wallace. He was an unassuming person, but he had an inner strength that the discerning quickly recognised. I remember him saying to the students: 'Small men are always defending themselves. They are not content to just make a point, but want to give endless reasons as to why they think the way they do. And if anyone disagrees with them or counters them they become almost fanatical in their defence of what they believe. Big men can always afford to wait for time to defend them.'

The defensive live more by fear than faith. The non-defensive are not afraid to confess to mistakes because, being essentially right (but not arrogantly so), they are never afraid to be sometimes wrong. How much simpler life is when free from defensiveness.

FURTHER STUDY

Luke 4:1–22; John 1:14; 6:63

1. Why were all the people amazed and spoke well of Jesus?

2. What were the elements of His glory that John beheld?

Lord Jesus Christ, teach me how to walk in Your footsteps and be, from this day forward, a less defensive person. Show me how to make a start this very hour. For Your own dear name's sake. Amen.

The divine perspective

FOR READING & MEDITATION – 1 CORINTHIANS 1:18–31

'Let him who boasts boast in the Lord.' (v31)

Yet another area of our life that Jesus simplified for us is that which has to do with the whole concept of success. We live in a time that has been labelled as 'The Success-Oriented Age' and people are captivated with the idea of being successful. The best-selling books are those with such titles as *How to Be a Success in Business, The Principles of Success, Why People Fail*, and so on.

Now let me say right away that I see nothing wrong in working to be successful, or in setting clear goals. I think the saying, 'People don't plan to fail but fail because they don't plan,' has some merit. But for a Christian there is much more to it than that. The most successful man who ever lived, our Lord Jesus Christ, failed by all the human standards that are used to measure success. He possessed no property, left no money, did not write a book, never established a headquarters or compiled a mailing list, and when He was taken by political and so-called spiritual leaders and crucified, most of His followers deserted Him. All He left were some simple seeds sown in the red furrows of men and women's hearts which, energised through the cross and resurrection, and watered by the Spirit, have spread throughout the earth and transformed the centuries.

A cartoon in a Good Friday edition of a newspaper I once saw had a drawing of Christ on the cross. The caption said 'Failure'. I crossed out the word 'Failure' and wrote in the word 'Success'. Only a divine perspective can help us distinguish the difference between success as the world sees it and success as God sees it.

FURTHER STUDY

Matt. 5:38–48; 23:11;
Luke 7:23–27;
John 12:24;
Acts 20:35

1. What are some biblical teachings that are contrary to modern thinking?

2. What would be the defensive way of dealing with these issues?

My Father and my God, help me move through life with my view shaped and guided by Your Word and not by the surrounding world-view. In Jesus' name I pray. Amen.

The tyranny of success

FOR READING & MEDITATION – 1 CHRONICLES 22:1–13

'Then you will have success if you are careful to observe the decrees and laws that the LORD gave' (v13)

We must move carefully through this issue of success as it is so easy to be misunderstood. Permit me once again to make clear that I am not condemning the drive to succeed or the need to establish clear goals and move forward to positive and successful ends. What I am seeking to raise a caution against is being driven by the idea of success, of being locked into the necessity of it. A good many people I know go through life nervously feeling the necessity of always succeeding. Their whole identity is caught up in it. If they succeed, they feel more than just successful, they feel complete as a person; if they fail, they feel destroyed. Their whole sense of personal identity hangs on the concept of success or failure.

But you do not have to succeed in everything you do. All you have to do is be true to what you believe God is leading you into, to pray with faith over every important issue, then success and failure are in the hands of God. That releases you from the tyranny of having to be successful. If you are always looking at the end and not at the means to the end, life becomes anxious and complex.

Act from this simple premise: pray about everything, do what is right, and leave the results to God. Trust that God has heard your prayer and will answer you. It might be a 'yes', a 'no' or a 'wait', but He will answer. Then the outcomes will always be right – in the long run.

You do not have to despise success, you simply must not depend on it. When God and His presence in your heart is the priority, then you can have it or do without it.

FURTHER STUDY

Josh. 1:1–9; 10:42; 11:23; 21:45; 24:31

1. What instructions did God give Joshua for success?

2. What was the overall result of Joshua's obedience?

Lord God, while I want to do well in what You want me to do, help me, however, not to be driven by the idea of having to be successful. Help me always do that which is right and trust the outcome to You. In Jesus' name. Amen.

God-given success

MON
9 OCT

FOR READING & MEDITATION – 2 CHRONICLES 26:1–23

'As long as [Uzziah] sought the LORD*, God gave him success.' (v5)*

Today's passage reminds us that as long as King Uzziah sought the Lord he had success. He experienced the best type of success – success that was God-given. As we can see from the record, however, once he became powerful, pride set in and led to his downfall. He thought he could take over from the priests and offer incense on the altar. When the priests confronted him he turned on them with fierce rage, whereupon God struck him with leprosy that remained upon him until the day he died.

What this passage tells us about success is that it is possible to build our life with God and then to allow that success to go to our heads. No one is free from this possibility. How many Christians have you heard of, or perhaps know, who clearly started out to do something with God, but pride set in and their lives were ruined? It must be kept in mind that we are never closer to failure than during the period of our greatest success. If we fail to recognise God's hand in our achievements, then they are no better than failures.

Those of you reading these lines who are sitting at this moment on the pinnacle of success, ask yourself this question: Am I in danger of overestimating my own importance in bringing about the achievements I have experienced? It is a dangerous moment when we discover that we can do many things well. If we are not careful, a consuming pride can invade us, like the leprous disease that invaded Uzziah's body. Never, never, never cease to give thanks to God for all your accomplishments. Give Him the credit for your success. After all, without Him you could do nothing.

FURTHER STUDY

2 Cor. 11:30; Phil. 4:10–13; 1 Cor. 1:27–29

1. How did Paul describe boasting about achievement?

2. Where was his dependency placed?

Father, forgive me if I have become self-dependent and carried away with my own accomplishments. I pause today to give You all the thanks for everything that You have given to me. In Jesus' name. Amen.

TUES
10 OCT

A formula for success

FOR READING & MEDITATION – PHILIPPIANS 4:1–10

'And the peace of God... will guard your hearts and your minds in Christ Jesus.' (v7)

We continue thinking through the issue of success as it relates to Christians. The age in which we live, we have been saying, is clearly success-oriented, and it is vital that we as Christians do not allow ourselves to be overly influenced by the world – a world, by the way, on which the prince of this world, Satan, has a strong and powerful grip. There is nothing wrong with ambition or with a desire to be successful provided these things are not the driving force that motivates us. It is better that we are weaned from the notion of the necessity of success before we achieve success, so that when it comes we know how to handle it.

I am aware that many business and professional people read *Every Day with Jesus* and I wouldn't want in any way to minimise the importance of enthusiasm and drive. But I would be less than faithful to my calling as a writer and a Bible teacher if I were to neglect drawing your attention to the need for constant reappraisal and self-examination as you move along the road towards success. I urge you to give as much attention to the means – prayer, meditation on the Scriptures and dependency on the Holy Spirit – as you do to the objective you are aiming for.

One businessman I know told me his formula for success was this: 'Early to bed, early to rise, work like crazy and advertise.' Today's passage gives a better one. Rejoice in God more than in what you accomplish. Never be anxious, because God is in final control. Pray about everything and never cease to be thankful. And let God's peace be the sentinel that stands on duty at the door of your heart.

FURTHER STUDY

Matt. 20:20–28; Luke 9:46–48; 10:17–20

1. What is often the result of personal ambition?

2. What did Jesus say His disciples were to rejoice about?

Loving heavenly Father, infuse these precious words from Scripture into my spirit so that they will become a guiding force in my life. Make me like a weaned child, weaned from all that complicates. In Jesus' name. Amen.

How to handle failure

FOR READING & MEDITATION – ROMANS 8:28–39

'And we know that in all things God works for the good of those who love him' (v28)

We have looked at how to handle success, but I also know some reading these lines will at this moment be more concerned with how to handle failure. Everything has seemingly gone wrong – your world has fallen apart. Perhaps your business venture has come unstuck, your marriage has failed, or something you started out to do for God has gone into reverse. You are discovering what a person once said – nothing recedes like success.

If failure is part of your life at this moment, then I suggest the following. First, be willing to accept the loss and don't shrink from the suffering it may cause you. Engage with the loss you feel, not with self-pity, but with a genuine willingness to experience the pain. It's by mourning a loss that you recover from it. Second, consider how you may have contributed to the failure. Look for any things in you that may have brought the situation to where it is. Decide to correct those things. You won't be able to put the clock back, but you can decide that you will learn from the situation and move into the future better equipped to deal with life. Where an apology is necessary, be ready to give it. And where forgiveness is needed, be prepared to offer it.

Third, surrender the whole situation into God's hands and take a fresh hold on the promise in our text today: 'all things work together for good to them that love God' (v28, KJV). When you are a Christian and you are fully committed to God, then you have Him at your side to help you turn the setbacks into springboards. And never forget that – painful though it may be to recognise it and admit it – you can learn more from failure than you can from success.

FURTHER STUDY

Psa. 51:1–19; 89:19–29

1. What was God's promise to David?

2. What steps did David take following his failure?

Father God, help me be alert and careful to listen to You, for when I listen to You, I listen to wisdom, goodness and redemption. Teach me the art of learning from my failures – learning what You want me to learn. In Jesus' name. Amen.

CWR in Singapore and Cambodia

We continue to be amazed at God's provision for us to teach Christian counselling and pastoral care courses in Singapore and Cambodia. He opens doors, guides our steps and grants us favour as we seek to serve the Church in South East Asia.

Our tutors have been teaching CWR's Waverley Integrative Framework (an approach to counselling, underpinned by a Christian anthropology) for many years in Singapore in various formats. Last year, we started teaching in Cambodia's capital city, Phnom Penh, which was an amazing opportunity to help a people in great need. Anna Clarkstone, one of our Waverley Abbey College tutors, describes what it was like:

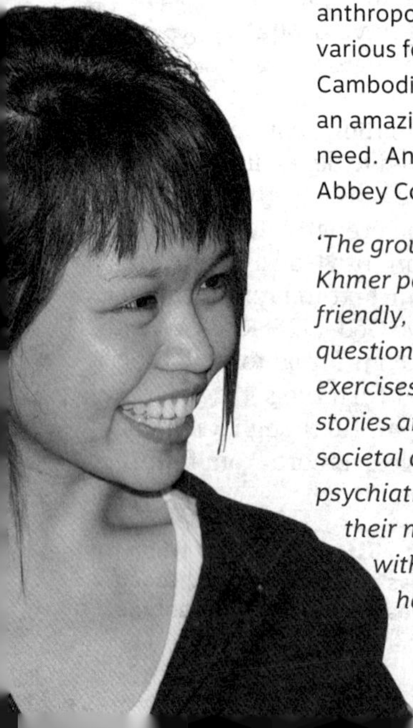

'The group of students was a mixture of local Khmer people and missionaries. They were friendly, attentive, gave feedback, asked questions and engaged very well with creative exercises and group work. They shared stories and educated us on their needs and societal differences; for example, there are no psychiatrists in Cambodia. We became aware of their need to process what they were learning within the class, as life is so busy that many have no time or spiritual space outside

the classroom. It was a challenge and steep learning curve for us to communicate in the best way for their learning.

I was also deeply struck by the endemic trauma experience of the people after the horrors of the Khmer Rouge. These students were all recovering from this terrible time. They are survivors, a generation of pioneers. Some came to know Jesus because of their loss and now speak to others and share testimonies of how the Lord has helped them. It is hard to fully understand their suffering. My hope is that learning in a group context and helping each other through the tools of the Waverley Integrative Framework are gifts in their hands.'

ANNA CLARKSTONE

By the end of October 2017, the full four modules of the Christian Counselling and Pastoral Care course will have been taught to students in both Singapore and Cambodia. The handbook for the modules has now been translated in both English and Khmer and the teaching team in Cambodia continues to grow. Please remember our students in Asia in your prayers, as well as the CWR tutors and local teams of teachers. We look forward to what God will do next.

Washing feet

FOR READING & MEDITATION – JOHN 13:1–17

'he poured water into a basin and began to wash his disciples' feet' (v5)

I have one more thing to say about the issue of success – learn to measure it by heavenly standards and not earthly ones. The American preacher Dr Paul Rees said: 'If you want a picture of success as heaven measures it, of greatness as God views it, don't look for the blaring of the bands on Broadway; listen rather for the tinkling of water splashing into a basin while God incarnate, in a humility that makes angels hold their breath, sponges the grime from the feet of His undeserving disciples.'

Earlier I said that Jesus Christ, the most successful man who ever lived, failed by all the earthly standards of success. Yet in the midst of what the world regards as failure, He achieved His greatest triumph. So learn to see failure from God's point of view. Can you see what this means? You don't always have to succeed! Your failure may contain within it the hidden seeds of future success. Dr J.B. Hawthorne, another great preacher and a powerful orator, once went to help a small church in an evangelistic outreach, and after two weeks' outreach only one young boy had given his life to Christ. Dr Hawthorne thought of himself as a failure, but the little boy who gave his heart to Christ in that mission grew up to be the noted A.T. Robertson, one of the greatest Greek scholars of the twentieth century.

FURTHER STUDY

Phil. 2:5–11; Matt. 20:28; Luke 22:27

1. What was the attitude of Christ?

2. What is more important than success?

Failure must always be viewed from the divine perspective. As Woodrow Wilson once put it, in words that have now become famous: 'I would rather fail in the cause that ultimately will triumph, than triumph in a cause that ultimately will fail.' That sums up the message of Christianity as well as anything I know.

Help me see success, Lord Jesus, from Your perspective. What the world sees as failure, You see as something different. Give me Your insight, Your wisdom, Your gaze at everything. Amen.

'The way to serve'

FOR READING & MEDITATION – JOHN 17:1–19

'I have brought you glory on earth by completing the work you gave me to do.' (v4)

Another area of life that seems to create complications for many people is that of commitment. There are so many things that need to be done, and so little time in which to accomplish them. How do we discharge our Christian duty and calling without falling into the trap of over-commitment?

Jesus beautifully simplified this area of life when He gave us the words of our verse today: 'I have brought you glory... by completing the work you gave me to do.' Note the word 'you'. There were many, including His disciples, who would have had Jesus running here, there, and everywhere in order to accomplish what they thought He should be doing, but He kept His heart open only to the things God required of Him. Thus, He was able to achieve more in three and a half years of ministry than many achieve in a lifetime.

When I was a young Christian, I used to hear people say: 'It is better to burn out than rust out. You are not serving the Lord unless you push yourself to the verge of exhaustion.' I was greatly influenced by that way of thinking in the early part of my discipleship, but I woke up one day, many years later, to see that it was not a biblical position at all. The trouble with the 'burn out or rust out' philosophy is that either way you're 'out', which, when you think about it, doesn't make much sense. I challenge anyone to find a page in the Gospels where Jesus appears to be over-committed. He moved through His ministry at a leisurely pace. Whatever He did, He did well, and He approached important issues with great seriousness. But He was never pressured. He modelled for us all the way in which we are to serve.

FURTHER STUDY

John 8:18–28; 6:14–15

1. Where did Jesus take His instructions from?

2. How did Jesus handle the pressure of the crowd?

Father, slow me down if I am going too fast. Show me that there is an option other than the 'burn out or rust out' philosophy. It is to do only what You want me to do. And I have all the time in the world for that. Amen.

SAT
14 OCT

'We are driven!'

FOR READING & MEDITATION – MARK 6:30–44

'Come with me by yourselves to a quiet place and get some rest.' (v31)

A statement I used to often hear when I was growing up was this: 'Cleanliness is next to godliness.' It seems to have been displaced in more recent days by the phrase: 'Exhaustion is next to godliness.' Many seem to think that the more exhausted Christians feel (and look!), the more committed they are to doing the work and will of God. Their favourite text is this: 'Jesus said... "My Father is always at his work to this very day, and I, too, am working"' (John 5:17).

When I see Christians overdoing things I often remember a car commercial in which a group of singers shouted: 'We are driven!' It is certainly true that Jesus was an enthusiastic worker, and sometimes, as we see from the incident at Jacob's Well at Sychar, He became tired (John 4:6), but there is never any suggestion in the Gospels that He became emotionally exhausted because of being over-committed. Never once do we see Him caught up in a frenzy of activity. Today's passage reveals Jesus deliberately seeking relief from the constant demand of ministering to others, and He advises His disciples to do the same. Our Lord's life was one of beautiful and simple balance. He accomplished everything the Father sent Him to do – everything – and He accomplished it without ignoring those essential times of rest and relaxation.

I realise that not all my readers will struggle with this difficulty, but I do notice warning signs in the Church that more and more believers are tending to see their identity in terms of their performance and their work. Unless we are careful, we will finish up being people who not only work at worship, but who worship work.

FURTHER STUDY

Luke 5:16; 9:10; Matt. 14:23; 15:29; 17:1; Gal. 6:9

1. What did Jesus often do?

2. What did Paul warn the Galatians against?

Lord Jesus, You whose life was a beautiful blend of activity and leisure, teach me this art also. Help me to know Your will for me, and to respond to the will of others only when it is Your will. In Jesus' name. Amen.

Balance – personified!

FOR READING & MEDITATION – LUKE 5:12–16

'But Jesus often withdrew to lonely places and prayed.' (v16)

Workaholics, 'churchaholics', over-committed believers – slow down. That is without doubt the message that comes to us both from the life of Christ and the teaching of the New Testament. So if you are caught up in moving through your responsibilities like an overloaded goods train then it's time to turn into a siding and pause for a few moments of self-examination. You have all the time to do what God wants you to do in this world – without fuss and without frenzy.

Those who, like me, were brought up indoctrinated with a strong work ethic, struggle with this because we have been hard-wired to believe that the more we do the more God loves us. I have been in bondage to this for most of my life, and only in recent years and with God's help have I been able to be free of it. I look back over the years and wonder how I ever allowed myself to get caught up in responding to requests for ministry that did not carry God's signature. It is because I learned the lesson of building a more balanced life rather late that I want to help you avoid that same mistake. How I wish someone had taken me aside early in my ministry and forced me to look in detail at the lifestyle of Jesus from the perspective I am talking about now. I certainly studied His life many times, but I looked only at the things He did and avoided looking at those occasions when He did nothing.

It is important not to get the impression from what I am now saying that Jesus strolled nonchalantly through His ministry. He was never aimless, half-hearted or discursive. But nor did He come anywhere near getting a heart attack. He was balance personified.

FURTHER STUDY

Isa. 40:25–31; Matt. 11:28; Heb. 12:3

1. What does Isaiah say is the antidote to weariness?

2. What has Jesus promised to the weary?

Son of God, reach deep into my soul today and give me such a sense of security that I will work because I am saved, not in order to be saved. And help me prevent that work becoming overwork. Amen.

Mimicking God

FOR READING & MEDITATION – EPHESIANS 5:1–21

'Be imitators of God, therefore, as dearly loved children' (v1)

What an intriguing command: 'Be imitators of God.' It's even stranger still when you realise the word 'imitators' comes from the Greek word *mimeomai*, from which we get the English word 'mimic'. Does it surprise you that we are being told to mimic God?

There are many ways, of course, in which we can imitate or mimic God, but the particular one I want to look at now is that which has to do with our present emphasis – developing a proper balance between activity and leisure. The very first being we read about in the Bible who took a rest is... God. He created – then rested. Many of you will have read, I'm sure, the opening chapters of Genesis. God created the heavens and the earth, fashioned the mountains, made the seas, and then, following the sixth day of creation, He stopped working. This is how the writer of Genesis puts it: 'By the seventh day God had finished the work he had been doing; so on the seventh day he rested from all his work. And God blessed the seventh day and made it holy, because on it he rested from all the work of creating that he had done' (Gen. 2:2–3).

Why did God rest on that seventh day? Because He was exhausted? No. Omnipotence does not get exhausted. Because there was nothing else for Him to do? No, not even that. He did it in order to set us an example. The Almighty knew full well that our creative times must be followed by restful times. We create – we rest. That is the way God has ordained things. Every one of us needs a regular and radical break from the routines of life, and if we are to be imitators or mimics of God then we must see to it that we too make rest a priority.

FURTHER STUDY

Psa. 62:1–12; 1 Kings 18:1–19:10

1. Where did the psalmist find his rest?

2. What were some of the elements that led to Elijah's exhaustion?

Dear Father, forgive me if I imitate You only in the area of work and creativity but not in the area of rest. You set me an example I must follow. Help me to honour You by imitating You. In Jesus' name. Amen.

Be still

FOR READING & MEDITATION – PSALM 46:1–11

'Be still, and know that I am God.' (v10)

How many times have you heard a parent say to an exuberant child: 'Be still'? Well, now your heavenly Father is saying the same thing to you! The famous French philosopher and Christian Pascal observed that most of our anxieties arise from the fact that we do not know how to sit in the middle of a room and just be still. I think that Pascal's advice is excellent, but I would go a step further and add: sit still in the presence of God.

Jesus knew how to be still. Time and time again we read of Him withdrawing from activity to commune quietly and privately with His heavenly Father. Every one of us must come to terms with the value of tranquillity, slowing down, moving apart from the hustle and bustle of life, and enriching our lives in quiet and deep communion with God. In fact, knowing God requires that we be still. 'Be still, and know that I am God.'

Does that mean we cannot know God in our times of activity? No, it is not saying that. The statement is designed to show us that when we spend time with God in the stillness, our heavenly Father has an opportunity to interact with us in ways that deepen our knowledge of Him and His ways. Then we are less likely to go off and involve ourselves in activities which are not for us to do. The more time we spend with God in the stillness, the more we will be able to say 'No' to those kind of activities that make us look as if we are getting somewhere when really we are not. So just in case you are rushing over these words, eager to get into the activities of the day, let me repeat what I have been trying to get across in my notes for today – knowing God requires that at times we be still.

FURTHER STUDY

1 Thess. 4:1–11; Prov. 17:1; Eccl. 4:6

1. What are we to make our ambition?

2. What is better: one handful or two?

Lord God, what a mistake it is when we allow ourselves to be slaves chained to schedules of our own making. Show us ways to break loose from that and the courage to put our world together in the way You want it to be. In Jesus' name. Amen.

Demonstration needed

FOR READING & MEDITATION – MATTHEW 6:25–34

'do not worry about tomorrow, for tomorrow will worry about itself.' (v34)

I suspect that over the past few days many heads have been nodding in recognition of what I have been saying about over-commitment. But you can nod your head until you get whiplash; it will do you no good unless you determine to act on what is being suggested. It is not inclination that is needed now, but demonstration. Here are some suggestions I hope will help.

First, decide to spend more time with God in prayer, endeavouring to know His will. Ask God to show you what things He wants you to be involved in and what things you need to simplify or stop. Many things in life are routine and you have to do them, but many things are not. List the big issues, bring them into your prayer time, and invite God to show you what you can do without.

Second, settle once and for all that your identity as a person is not found in your work but in who you are in God. Work is important (don't hear me minimising it), but that is not the primary source of your identity. You are who you are because of your relationship with Jesus Christ. You might one day have to stop working, yet that will make no difference to the fact that you are His child. Always remember that.

Third, build into your schedule definite times for leisure and relaxation. You are called to imitate God, so start by imitating Him in relation to this matter of leisure and rest. Jesus did it, and so must we. There is much more to life than work. Make yourself aware of the beautiful sights and sounds of the world that God has wrapped around us. Believe me, if you decide to do what I suggest, five years from now you will look back to this day and be glad you gave your schedules, activities and plans into your heavenly Father's hands.

FURTHER STUDY

Psa. 143:1–10; 40:8; James 4:13–15

1. What did the psalmist pray?

2. What are we to say?

Loving heavenly Father, may we become people like Your Son – committed to You, working for You, yet relaxed and leisurely in our approach to life. Help us enjoy life, not simply endure it. In Christ's name we pray. Amen.

Dealing with temptation

FOR READING & MEDITATION – MATTHEW 4:1–11

'Jesus said... "it is written..." Then the devil left him' (vv10–11)

An area of life that Jesus once again so beautifully simplified is that which has to do with the matter of temptation. Now of course temptation can be an extremely complex issue, and is one that can sometimes cause people great distress and consternation. In no way do I want to be guilty of oversimplifying it. But there is nothing complex about the manner in which we can deal with temptation. This has been made clear and simple by the example of Jesus Himself. Let me also remind you at the outset that temptation is not sin.

Turn again to today's passage. Jesus was presented with three persuasive and powerful propositions. First, He was tempted to turn stones into bread. At the end of a 40-day fast, you can imagine how appealing this idea could have been. But Jesus saw it as a scam to shift His gaze away from the face of the Father. Second, He was taken to the holy city and, standing there on the highest point of the Temple, was invited to throw Himself down and test the Father's willingness to protect Him from physical harm. Again He saw right through this strategy as an attempt to prove something He already knew was true. If you really believe something to be true, you don't need to have it proved. Third, Satan, whom Jesus sometimes referred to as 'The prince of this world', offered Him a shortcut to the kingdoms of the earth. He said in effect: 'Bow down to me and you won't have to fight me for them; I will give them to you.'

How did Jesus handle these complex issues? He did not engage in mental tricks or resort to some complicated formula. He resorted to the precise words of Scripture. Could anything be more simple?

FURTHER STUDY

1 Cor. 10:1–13; Heb. 2:18

1. What has God promised when we are tempted?

2. What are we to be careful about?

Lord Jesus, help me understand that leaning only on my own words I am no match for Satan. But when Your Word is in my heart and the right word is on my lips, then he is no match for me. For Your own dear name's sake. Amen.

Two kinds of power

FOR READING & MEDITATION – PSALM 23:1–6

'he restores my soul.' (v3)

We saw yesterday how Jesus handled the temptations in the wilderness by depending on Scripture. He immediately used the Word of God. We should keep in mind, also, that it was the only rebuttal He used, even though He could have turned to other resources available to Him – miracles, angels, prayer, and so on. Of all His resources, He chose only to lean on the Scripture given to Him specifically for this occasion. Note the word 'specifically', for this is the key to handling temptation. It is not enough to know a few verses of the Bible. We soak our minds in Scripture so that we are able to select the right word for the right occasion.

John Sherrill, one-time editor of *Guideposts* magazine and a prolific writer, says that in his study of the Bible he has noticed there are certain verses that seem imbued with an unusual power. These, he claims, can be divided into two types – manna verses and arsenal verses. A manna verse is a verse on which we can regularly feed and draw deep inspiration or encouragement; an arsenal verse is a verse that we store in our memories to use when we find ourselves encountering some fierce temptation or an attack of Satan. The well-known psalm in today's reading contains both, according to Sherrill. The verse, 'The LORD is my shepherd, I shall lack nothing,' is a manna verse on which we can feed over and over again. The phrase, 'he restores my soul,' is an arsenal verse that can be leaned on when one feels overcome by temptation.

What energy and power lies hidden in the Word of God. If we ignore this God-given resource to help us resist temptation, we are living dangerously.

FURTHER STUDY

Gen. 3:1–24; 2 Cor. 11:3; 2:11

1. What did Satan do to the truth God had given Adam and Eve?

2. What was Paul's concern for the Corinthians?

My Father and my God, what a provision You have given me in Your Word – manna verses, arsenal verses, and many other kinds also. Help me soak my mind in Scripture so that it becomes my very energy and life. In Jesus' name I pray. Amen.

Next Issue

NOV/DEC 2017

The God of All Comfort

We all at times experience discomfort or pain, whether it be physical or emotional. Many struggle to determine where this comes from, and why.

Written from Selwyn's personal experience, this issue unfolds how the God of all comfort can help turn the problem of seemingly purposeless pain into something positive when we hand it over to Him. Selwyn uses examples such as loneliness, bereavement and shattered dreams to explore how, as we draw near to God, He comforts us and makes us whole.

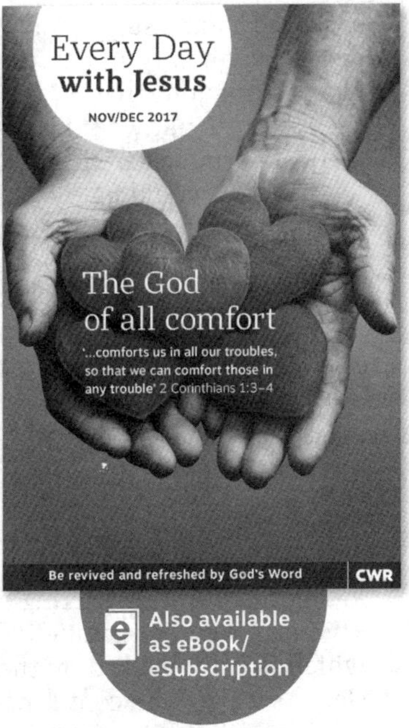

Also available as eBook/ eSubscription

Obtain your copy from CWR, a Christian bookshop or National Distributor.
If you would like to take out a subscription, see the order form at the back of these notes.

SAT 21 OCT

The infallible Word of God

FOR READING & MEDITATION – GENESIS 3:1–13

'God did say, "You must not eat fruit from the tree that is in the middle of the garden"' (v3)

Of all the insights I have gained in studying the Bible, one of the most powerful is the principle of resisting temptation by using God's written Word. Jesus (as we have seen) demonstrated this so beautifully and simply in His encounter with Satan in the wilderness. Three times in a row He faced His trials by referring Satan to the infallible Word of God. He shredded Satan's suggestions by aiming one perfect word at the deception and argument, then releasing its incredible power by speaking it forth.

FURTHER STUDY

James 1:1–12; Eph. 6:13–18

1. What does Paul encourage the Ephesians to do when evil comes?

2. How many pieces of armour does Paul list to stand firm in?

What would have happened if Eve had used this principle in the Garden of Eden? One thing is certain – I would not be writing these lines at the moment, for, if Adam and Eve had obeyed the spoken Word of God that they had been given, then there would have been no need for a written Word. And thus no need for Bible notes or Bible expositors. What Eve could have done was to refuse to budge from the clear statement that God had made: 'You must not eat fruit from the tree that is in the middle of the garden.' As you can see from today's reading, she did actually draw Satan's attention to it, but allowed herself to be moved away from God when she listened to the serpent's suggestion that He might have a less than loving motive in restricting them in this way.

We can resist temptation, then, by the truth of God's Word, which is fully backed by the whole nature and character of God. As we grow in confidence in His Word and His redeeming love, we will more quickly recognise the lies and deceptions of the evil one. This in turn enables us to turn more quickly to the truth and love and safety of our heavenly Father.

Gracious God, give me, I pray, an unshakable confidence in the power and veracity of Your Word. Teach me how to doubt my doubts and believe my beliefs. Build my faith so that I cannot be shaken by Satan. Help me, my Father. Amen.

'All' means 'all'

FOR READING & MEDITATION – 2 TIMOTHY 3:1–16

'All Scripture is God-breathed' (v16)

We said yesterday that although the best method of dealing with Satan's temptations is to refer him to the words of Scripture, more is needed if the temptation is to be overcome. This is the point I want to develop still further with you today. It is not enough to select an appropriate passage to aim at the devil – we must link ourselves to it in absolute trust and believe it to be the eternal Word of God.

Now this is supremely important, because many have slipped up here. They have thought all they needed to do was to select an appropriate verse of Scripture, aim it at Satan, and watch the Word do its work. If this is all that is involved, then Eve would have been able to resist the serpent's suggestions, and there would have been no Fall. The devil, however, saw, and no doubt sensed by the way she had repeated the statement, that she was open to doubt. Then, Satan followed up on that with an intuitive sense and insight, that was so cunning, sharp and formidable that he was able to push her towards that first cataclysmic violation.

One of my concerns about many in today's Church who cast doubts on the authority and veracity of the Scriptures, is that in that position they are quite defenceless when it comes to spiritual warfare. Satan has them at his mercy. They may quote the Word of God, but if they don't believe it to be inspired and authoritative, then they are easy prey for the adversary. I urge those reading these lines who, although committed to Christ, do not have a high view of Scripture, to think again. God has told us: 'All Scripture is breathed out by God' (v16, ESV). All!

FURTHER STUDY

2 Pet. 1:1–21; 2 Tim. 3:16; Col. 3:16

1. Where did Scripture have its origin?

2. What did Paul encourage the Colossians to do?

Dear Father, once again I ask, help me have confidence in the Bible. If there are doubts deep within me, help me clear them up so that I come to a place of absolute trust and dependency on Your Word. In Jesus' name. Amen.

'Say so!'

FOR READING & MEDITATION – PSALM 107:1–16

'Let the redeemed of the LORD say this' (v2)

There is just one more lesson I want to draw from the example of Jesus' dismissal of Satan during His temptations in the wilderness and it is this – Christ took the Word of God, applied it to Himself, believed it implicitly, and spoke it out loud.

There is a teaching known as 'Positive Confession', which (in my opinion) takes this idea of speaking the Word of God out loud to extremes. There is, nevertheless, a clear biblical foundation for letting God's Word pass not only through our minds but over our lips. 'And God said, "Let there be light," and there was light' (Gen. 1:3). 'If you confess with your mouth, "Jesus is Lord"... you will be saved' (Rom. 10:9). To confess in this sense is to 'say with God'. When I confess God's Word, I am pronouncing His own Word with Him. Then again, we read in the Psalms: 'For he spoke, and it came to be; he commanded, and it stood firm' (Psa. 33:9).

I don't quite know how it works, but there is power to be experienced in speaking the Word of God out loud. I have witnessed this power in my own life many times, and in the lives of others also. Of course, critics of this idea point out that Jesus wasn't the only one who spoke out the Word of God in the temptation in the wilderness. Satan did too. Obviously, the difference was that the Word spoken by Satan was the wrong Word for the occasion and used to deceive; the Word uttered by Christ was the right Word for the occasion and spoken to uphold the glory of God. Satan knows how to build an argument, but he has no defence against the Christian who knows the Word, believes the Word, and is committed to the Word. Simple!

FURTHER STUDY

Rom. 10:1–10; Phil. 2:11; Heb. 3:1; 13:15

1. What major truth are we to confess with our mouths?
2. What will every tongue have to confess one day?

Lord Jesus, I recognise that my sinful nature likes to have a hand in my defence and longs to come up with something a little more complex – something I can take pride in. Deliver me from this. In Jesus' name. Amen.

A more excellent way

FOR READING & MEDITATION – JOHN 5:31–47

'You diligently study the Scriptures because you think that by them you possess eternal life.' (v39)

The danger we face when temptation comes our way is to rely more on our own initiative or mental agility than on the Word of God. I find it deeply challenging that when Jesus was tempted in the wilderness He did not try clever mental manoeuvres, or repeat trite sound bites like, 'When the going gets tough, the tough get going.' No one has ever been more mentally astute or had a keener mind than Jesus. If in the heat of fierce temptation He resorted to quoting the precise words of Scripture – and only to that – then how much more should we?

As we said briefly yesterday, it appeals to our old nature to come up with all kinds of mental tricks to deal with temptation. These ideas tend to feed our ego. I have read many intriguing and complicated formulae for dealing with temptation, and while I am not prepared to say they have no value at all, there can be little doubt that the best way is to follow the example of Jesus and go right back to the clear words of Scripture. God's Word is imperishable, unimpeachable, and infallible.

As a preacher and a writer, I have been attempting for most of my life to explain the vitality of God's Word. Even though I still cannot do so fully, there is an energy flowing through the words God has brought together in Scripture that is not to be found in any other book. This is not to say that some other books do not carry the stamp of His inspiration, but there is no book in the world that has quite the power of the Bible. And I am prepared to say that unless we spend time with this Book and soak our minds in its truth, then however clever we are, we are no match for Satan at the time of temptation.

FURTHER STUDY

John 8:31–47; Psa. 119:9;

1. What did Jesus say happens when we know the truth?

2. How did He describe the devil?

Father, I am grateful for Christian writings, but I see I must be careful not to measure the Scriptures by these; I must measure these by the Scriptures. Help me always to do this. In Christ's name I pray. Amen.

Life is for loving

FOR READING & MEDITATION – MARK 12:28–34

'love [God] with all your heart... and... love your neighbour as yourself' (v33)

The last area of life we look at that Jesus so beautifully simplified has to do with the whole purpose of living. Throughout time philosophers and thinkers have wrestled with the question of why we are here, and have come to a variety of conclusions. 'Life is for living,' said one great philosopher. By that he meant we are here to enjoy ourselves as best as we can, to sample something of the pleasures the world has on offer, and then pass out into oblivion. Others have come up with far more complicated theories. In today's reading we see Jesus once again simplifying the whole matter and telling us in a single word what life is all about. Life is for loving, says Jesus. We are here to love God, and to love others. I ask you – could anything be simpler?

I once described the importance of love to a group of people. Afterwards a man came up to me and said: 'Love is the homeland of my soul; love is my native air.' I commented: 'That's a beautiful way to describe it. What made you put it like that?' He replied: 'Because in the atmosphere of love you can breathe deeply, breathe fully, breathe all the way down.' I pondered on his words and came up with some thoughts of my own.

Love is the atmosphere for which we were made. When we breathe in love, God's love, and give it out, we are functioning in the way we were designed. That is why being in a loveless atmosphere makes us feel choked, stifled. Little children who are not loved develop all kinds of problems – physical, mental, and spiritual. If love makes the world go round, lovelessness is what stops it spinning.

FURTHER STUDY

John 15:1–9, 13; Matt. 22:39;

1. What was Jesus able to say to His disciples?
2. What did He encourage them to do?

Father, I see so clearly that having been made in Your image – love – we are made by love and for love. And when we find love, we find everything, for love glorifies all. Help me fulfil my destiny. In Jesus' name. Amen.

'The Great Simplicity'

FOR READING & MEDITATION – HEBREWS 10:19–31

'And let us consider how we may spur one another on towards love and good deeds.' (v24)

We said yesterday that living is loving, and that love is the homeland of our soul, our native air. Without love we suffer from a kind of nostalgia that affects our spirits, our souls and our bodies.

I once heard a man, a medical doctor, say that while he was having a meal with some friends he sensed there was an absence of love among them and announced: 'I'm sorry I cannot stay. My digestion will give me trouble if I do.' He went on to say that lovelessness hinders digestion, dries up the gastric juices, and that if you want to digest your food then you must take love to the table with you. He talked of an experiment during which observers watched the process of digestion through an opening in a man's stomach. They found that when the man was in good humour, 'his digestion was normal, his stomach blushed a rosy red, and the gastric juices poured down like sweat on one's face.' But the moment he became angry, the colour of his stomach changed, the gastric juices stopped flowing and his digestive system was thrown into chaos. Clearly, the body is made for love, just like the soul.

For many years I have been a student of the Scriptures and of people, and I am convinced that to act on love is realism – the only realism. To act on anything but love is to complicate issues and introduce a disruptive tendency which, sooner or later, ties a situation in knots. Inherently, everything is made to work in love's way, and in no other way. If we try to make life work in any other way than love we work our own ruin. Love has been described as 'the Great Simplicity'. By that standard lovelessness is 'the Great Complexity'.

FURTHER STUDY

Rom. 12:9–10; 13:8–10; 1 Thess. 3:12

1. What must love be?

2. What was Paul's desire for the Thessalonians?

God my Father, You have made us in such a way that to love is the only way to live. Help us not to be driven to love by necessity, but help us to choose love. Help me love as You love, dear Father. In Jesus' name. Amen.

Love can't fail

FOR READING & MEDITATION – 1 CORINTHIANS 13:1–13

'Love never fails.' (v8)

Listen to the words again: 'Love never fails.' Never. Is this really true? What about when you love someone and that person turns away from you? What about the situation when a child rejects loving and caring parents? Or, when a husband or wife continues to love an unfaithful partner only to find that partner asking for a divorce to marry someone else? What's the answer?

It is this – to say that love never fails is not the same as saying it will always succeed in bringing about change in its object. If that were true then everybody will eventually be saved. Paul, in making this statement, is not saying: 'Love will never fail in winning the object of its desire.' What he is saying is this – when you act on love then, even though you may not gain what you hoped you might gain, you have not failed, for you have put a deposit into the situation that works in ways that are completely unknown to you. For one thing, you yourself are the better for acting on the basis of love. And so are those who are the recipients of your love. They may not feel it at the moment, but something is working in their lives that is positive and good. On one occasion, Jesus told His disciples when entering a home to offer peace to the people of the house. If they don't receive it, He said, then 'let your peace return to you' (Matt. 10:13). If they take it, good; if they don't take it, then it is still good. You are more peaceful for having given the peace.

The loving person always wins because, not least, he or she becomes the more loving for giving out love. 'Love never fails' – never fails to enrich the giver of love. It just can't fail. And for the same reason, the unloving act can never succeed.

FURTHER STUDY

1 Pet. 1:1–22; 1 John 3:16

1. How are we to love each other?

2. How do we know what love is?

Father, since love is the victory, then I cannot fail if I love. Help me to practise love today. I ask this in Jesus' name. Amen.

More precious than gold

SAT
28 OCT

FOR READING & MEDITATION – 1 JOHN 2:1–14

'But if anyone obeys his word, God's love is truly made complete in him.' (v5)

We ended yesterday with the statement: 'the unloving act can never succeed.' If you should succeed in getting your way by an unloving attitude or deed, you won't really be succeeding, not in the true sense of the word, because the unloving attitude or deed registers itself in you, becomes you. In other words, instead of gaining an advantage over someone else you will find yourself diminished by the unloving attitude or deed.

A woman who was always intent on changing people in a certain church (you could tell her victims by their 'hunted' look) listened to a sermon brought by a visiting minister, and she saw just where she had been going wrong. This is what she wrote to a friend some time later: 'The amazing thing was that I had been so concerned as to how I could transform everyone else, and then suddenly, as I looked at them through the eyes of Jesus, they all looked wonderful and already transformed. How right the preacher was about everyone being an island and needing love. When one finds Jesus, He does the transforming from the inside out. We are not capable of changing anyone. But to love them and help them find Him is the answer.' What a simple remedy. She, who had been trying to change others, was herself changed by the love of Jesus within. Then, as she viewed people through His eyes and His love, they looked different – they were changed without her trying to change them.

FURTHER STUDY

Rom. 8:28–37; Jer. 31:3; Eph. 2:4–5

1. What question does Paul ask?

2. What conclusion does he come to?

Love transforms everything it touches and everything it sees. You have heard of the Midas touch, in which everything touched turned to gold; this is the Master's touch, which turns everything into something more precious than gold.

Dear Lord, You who were incarnate love, show me how to love with Your love. Then ugliness will be turned into beauty, littleness into greatness, and pettiness into significance. Help me not to try to change people – just to love them. Amen.

Faith that 'works'

FOR READING & MEDITATION – GALATIANS 5:1–10

'The only thing that counts is faith expressing itself through love.' (v6)

There are some who believe that faith is the energy that enables Christianity. But it is not – what enables Christianity is faith that 'works by love' (Authorised Version phrase). Most who profess to be Christians have faith, but with many, their faith does not 'work by love', it works by fear, by combat, and by aggressiveness towards those who do not see eye to eye with them. Their faith works, but not in the Bible way.

Why is it that so many Christians feel their faith needs defending? The Christian faith does not need protection, it needs proclamation. It is its own defence. The sun doesn't need protection because someone throws mud at it; the sun shines no matter what, and is its own protection. There are far too many anxious Christians in the Church who go about trying to steady the Ark, and end up not dead as Uzzah did (2 Sam. 6:7), but in dead trouble. If they would go out and love, that would be protection for the Christian faith, for it would be a proclamation of the Christian faith. Our faith works out through love because that is the only way it can work. Love is the applied edge of the Christian faith, or, as it's been said: the place where the rubber meets the road. I heard a preacher say once: 'Faith is love in shoes. It goes out to serve – the least, the last, and the lost.'

When our faith works by love then it shows we have faith in love. If we go down loving then we go down, but we will not stay down. For love, as we have been saying, never fails. It is love or nothing. Anger or force cannot compensate where love is failing. Everything that has no love in it is ultimately bound to fail.

FURTHER STUDY

John 13:1–35; Gal. 5:22–23

1. What evangelism plan did Jesus give to His disciples?

2. What is the fruit of the Spirit and how is it evidenced?

Father, it is becoming clearer each day – I must follow the pathway of love. Help me to make love my motive, my method, my atmosphere and my goal. Then if nothing happens on the outside I know something will happen on the inside. Amen.

The world's sickness

FOR READING & MEDITATION – 1 JOHN 4:7–21

'if we love one another, God lives in us and his love is made complete in us.' (v12)

We have been saying these past few days that living is loving. That simple formula was presented to us by Jesus, and the ages have come to see how true it is. In his book *Love against Hate* Karl Menninger says: 'The psychologist speaking for science is like a voice crying in the wilderness... The disease of the world is the disease of the individual personality... and the World War of today is a reflection of the multiple wars in the hearts of individuals.' Powerful words. If the sickness of the world is the sickness of the individual, and if the sickness of the individual is lack of love, then the sickness of the world is lack of love. Therefore the world, out of sheer necessity, is being driven back to the simple message of Jesus – living is loving.

Love is not an elective course in the school of life; it is a must. It can be said that many people's problems come from the fact that society has not fully grasped that 'It is more blessed to give than to receive' (Acts 20:35). Jesus made that simple statement close on 2,000 years ago, and now science comes along and says: 'If you don't understand that you don't know how to live.'

So if you evaluate Jesus' lifestyle through the door of science or the door of Scripture you come out at the same place – love. Only to the extent that we love do we live. Show me a church that has love in it and I will show you people who know how to live – really live. Where love is, there is the true Church, and where love is, there go the truest Christians. And nothing, absolutely nothing, can compensate for the lack of it. We live only when we love.

FURTHER STUDY

Col. 3:1–14;
1 Cor. 13:13;
Eph. 5:2;
1 John 4:16

1. What kind of life did Paul encourage?

2. What is happening when we live in love?

Father, I cannot love in my own strength. I can only love effectively when I love with Your love. So I open my heart now to the flow of Your love. Come and live in me, then I know You will also love in me. In Jesus' name I ask it. Amen.

One responsibility

FOR READING & MEDITATION – JOHN 15:1–17

'If you remain in me... ask whatever you wish, and it will be given you.' (v7)

On this our last day together of exploring the 'way of simplicity', it's amazing to think that on 31 October 1517 Martin Luther began the great Reformation that brought the Church back to a simple faith in Christ and the Bible as its authority. We too now ask ourselves: What are the implications of following Jesus in simplicity?

We remind ourselves that we do not need to be dependent on material possessions because we know the source of all things – Christ Himself. Some people always want more, but when you know Jesus, really know Him, you can learn to rely on Him and live on simple pleasures, simple loves and simple things, neither despising possessions, nor depending on them.

In Him we also understand real success. We learn to simply sow the seeds of love and truth, and then watch them bring forth fruit of their own accord. The successes of life are experienced mainly through the simplicities of life. Alexander Maclaren once preached a whole series of sermons to win a noted agnostic to Christ. At last, the man was won, but not through Maclaren's great preaching. The turning point came when the agnostic helped an old woman down the steps of the church, and she turned to him and said: 'Oh thank you so much. Do you love Jesus Christ my Saviour too? He means all the world to me.' Simplicity won where learning failed.

My one responsibility to live a fruitful life in the 'simplicity that is in Christ' is summed up so clearly and simply by the prophet Micah: 'To act justly and to love mercy and to walk humbly with your God' (6:8). So simple, yet so sublime.

FURTHER STUDY

John 17:1–23; 1 John 2:28; 3:6

1. What did Jesus say concerning the world knowing about Him?

2. What areas of Christ's simplicity do you need to incorporate in your own life?

My Father and my God, life has been so complex and complicated and now, at long last, I am coming to the simple. Help me live out my union with You in joyful, childlike faith, yet also growing in my understanding of all that You are. Amen.

Order form

EDWJ S/O 2017

4 Easy Ways To Order

1. Phone in your credit card order: **01252 784700** (Mon–Fri, 9.30am – 5pm)
2. Visit our online store at **www.cwr.org.uk/store**
3. Send this form together with your payment to: **CWR, Waverley Abbey House, Waverley Lane, Farnham, Surrey GU9 8EP**
4. Visit a Christian bookshop

For a list of our National Distributors, who supply countries outside the UK, visit **www.cwr.org.uk/distributors**

Your Details (required for orders and donations)

Full Name:	**CWR ID No.** (if known):
Home Address:	
	Postcode:
Telephone No. (for queries):	**Email:**

Publications

TITLE	QTY	PRICE	TOTAL
Total Publications			
UK P&P: up to £24.99 = **£2.99**; £25.00 and over = **FREE**			
Elsewhere P&P: up to £10 = **£4.95**; £10.01 – £50 = **£6.95**; £50.01 – £99.99 = **£10**; £100 and over = **£30**			
Total Publications and P&P (please allow 14 days for delivery)		**A**	

All CWR adult Bible reading notes are also available in **eBook** and **email subscription** format. Visit **www.cwr.org.uk** for further information.

Subscriptions* (non direct debit)	QTY	PRICE (including P&P) UK	Europe	Elsewhere	TOTAL
Every Day with Jesus (1yr, 6 issues)		£15.95	£19.95	Please contact nearest National Distributor or CWR direct	
Large Print *Every Day with Jesus* (1yr, 6 issues)		£15.95	£19.95		
Inspiring Women Every Day (1yr, 6 issues)		£15.95	£19.95		
Life Every Day (Jeff Lucas) (1yr, 6 issues)		£15.95	£19.95		
Mettle: 15–18s (1yr, 3 issues)		£14.50	£16.60		
YP's: 11–14s (1yr, 6 issues)		£15.95	£19.95		
Topz: 7–11s (1yr, 6 issues)		£15.95	£19.95		
Cover to Cover Every Day	Email subscription only, to order visit online store.				
Total Subscriptions (subscription prices already include postage and packing)				**B**	

Please circle which issue you would like your subscription to commence from:

JAN/FEB MAR/APR MAY/JUN JUL/AUG SEP/OCT NOV/DEC *Mettle* **JAN–APR MAY–AUG SEP–DEC**

*Only use this section for subscriptions paid for by credit/debit card or cheque. For Direct Debit subscriptions see overleaf.

We promise to never share your details with other charities. By giving us your personal information, you agree that we may use this to send you information about the ministry of CWR. If you do not want to receive further information by post, please tick here. ☐

Continued overleaf >>

<< See previous page for start of order form

Payment Details

☐ I enclose a cheque/PO made payable to CWR for the amount of: £ ____________

☐ Please charge my credit/debit card.

Cardholder's Name (in BLOCK CAPITALS) ____________

Card No. ☐☐☐☐ ☐☐☐☐ ☐☐☐☐ ☐☐☐☐

Expires End ☐☐ ☐☐ Security Code ☐☐☐

Gift to CWR

☐ Please send me an acknowledgement of my gift **C** ☐

Gift Aid (your home address required, see overleaf)

giftaid it

I am a UK taxpayer and want CWR to reclaim the tax on all my donations for the four years prior to this year **and on** all donations I make from the date of this Gift Aid declaration until further notice.*

Taxpayer's Full Name (in BLOCK CAPITALS) ____________

Signature ____________ **Date** ____________

*I am a UK taxpayer and understand that if I pay less Income Tax and/or Capital Gains Tax than the amount of Gift Aid claimed on all my donations in that tax year it is my responsibility to pay any difference.

GRAND TOTAL (Total of A, B & C) ☐

Subscriptions by Direct Debit (UK bank account holders only)

One-year subscriptions cost £15.95 (except *Mettle*: £14.50) and include UK delivery. Please tick relevant boxes and fill in the form below.

☐ *Every Day with Jesus* (1yr, 6 issues)
☐ Large Print *Every Day with Jesus* (1yr, 6 issues)
☐ *Inspiring Women Every Day* (1yr, 6 issues)
☐ *Life Every Day* (Jeff Lucas) (1yr, 6 issues)
☐ *Mettle*: 15–18s (1yr, 3 issues)
☐ *YP's*: 11–14s (1yr, 6 issues)
☐ *Topz*: 7–11s (1yr, 6 issues)

Issue to commence from

☐ Jan/Feb ☐ Jul/Aug *Mettle* ☐ Jan–Apr
☐ Mar/Apr ☐ Sep/Oct ☐ May–Aug
☐ May/Jun ☐ Nov/Dec ☐ Sep–Dec

CWR **Instruction to your Bank or Building Society to pay by Direct Debit**

DIRECT Debit

Please fill in the form and send to: CWR, Waverley Abbey House, Waverley Lane, Farnham, Surrey GU9 8EP

Name and full postal address of your Bank or Building Society

To: The Manager Bank/Building Society

Address

Postcode

Name(s) of Account Holder(s)

Branch Sort Code

Bank/Building Society Account Number

Originator's Identification Number

4	2	0	4	8	7

Reference

Instruction to your Bank or Building Society

Please pay CWR Direct Debits from the account detailed in this Instructio[n] subject to the safeguards assured by the Direct Debit Guarantee. I understand that this Instruction may remain with CWR and, if so, details will be passed electronically to my Bank/Building Society.

Signature(s)

Date

Banks and Building Societies may not accept Direct Debit Instructions for some types of account